CAN RELIGIOUS LIFE BE PROPHETIC?

CAN RELIGIOUS LIFE BE PROPHETIC?

Michael H. Crosby, OFMCap.

A Crossroad Book
The Crossroad Publishing Company
New York

Nihil Obstat:
Rev. Francis Dombrowski, OFMCap., S.T.L.
  Provincial Censor of Books
  September 4, 2004
Very Rev. Daniel Anholzer, OFMCap.
  Provincial Minister
  Province of St. Joseph of the Capuchin Order
  September 4, 2004.

The Crossroad Publishing Company
16 Penn Plaza, 481 Eighth Avenue
New York, NY 10001

Printed in the United States of America

This text of this book is set in 11/14.5 Goudy Old Style.
The display faces are Goudy Handtooled, Isadora, and Charlemagne.

Library of Congress Cataloging-in-Publication Data

Crosby, Michael, 1940-
    Can religious life be prophetic? / Michael H. Crosby.
       p.   cm.
    Includes bibliographical references.
    ISBN 0-8245-2270-2 (alk. paper)
       1. Christian life – Catholic authors. 2. Prophecy – Christianity.
    3. Catholic Church – Doctrines. I. Title.
    BX2350.3.C76 2005
    255 – dc22

                                                    2005000340

2   3   4   5   6   7   8   9   10   10   09   08   07   06

Contents

Introduction

Prophetic Proclamation in a Church Constitutively Clerical

The Rationale for and Structure of This Book

In 2002 I presented my reflections on "Prophetic Voices" to members of six congregations of Franciscan sisters. All traced their original roots to the Sisters of St. Francis of Philadelphia, founded by St. John Neumann and Mother Francis Bachmann. Due in part to the interference of bishops where the sisters had established foundations, the Philadelphia entity gave rise to other foundations: two in the Pittsburgh area (Millvale and Whitehall) and three in New York (Hastings-on-Hudson, Syracuse, and Buffalo).

When first asked to speak on the theme, I accepted, thinking I could simply reach into my files and present materials on prophecy and religious life I had previously presented.[1] However, the more the media reported stories of corporate malfeasance, political subservience to corporations, child sexual abuse by pedophile priests, and systemic abuses of power exercised by some major leaders in the hierarchy, my assigned topic, considering religious as "prophetic voices" in the midst of such injustice, became all the more challenging. I began to realize that I needed to rethink my entire approach to the topic. Around the same time, in June 2002, there arose a conflict between my Midwest Province of Capuchin Franciscans and the Vatican that convinced me of the need to view the issue of "prophetic voices" with a totally new lens.

At our Provincial Chapter that year we elected Robert Smith, a perpetually professed lay brother, as our minister provincial after serious and extended discussions, even though we knew full well that the Vatican had not approved "brothers-as-provincials" in other provinces of the order. Indeed, the minister general of the order told us that even if we elected him at our meeting in Detroit, Rome would almost certainly not accept our discernment. Nevertheless, knowing the institutional obstacles, we prayed to the Holy Spirit for guidance. Then we voted. We elected Smith on the first ballot by an overwhelming majority and, as expected, our decision was rejected by the Congregation for Institutes of Consecrated Life and Scieties of Apostolic Life (CICLSAL). The only reason for the rejection had nothing to do with Smith's qualifications, except for one: he was not an ordained priest.

Ignoring the irony that Francis of Assisi founded us as a community in which the charism of leadership would be open to all, the Vatican would not accept a nonordained brother because this meant a layman would have jurisdiction over clerics.

During our discussions some suggested we devise ways to sidestep a rejection of our choice by the CICLSAL. One said: "Let's ordain him." Another proposed the possibility of electing as provincial a member of the council who was a priest and to name Robert Smith our president. The minister general strongly opposed such a move because it might lead Rome to suppress the whole order. Intimidated by such a threat, stymied in finding a creative way of challenging the decision, and unable to find a nonviolent alternative, our province capitulated to the decision. Any prophetic action we might have taken was crushed by the clerical control of the Curia.

With this incident fresh in my mind, I arrived in Syracuse, where the Neumann/Bachmann group had gathered, knowing my topic would not be so simple to address. Indeed, I had also concluded that any reflections I might offer about us religious being "prophetic voices" in the midst of the injustice and oppression occurring in our church and culture would not fall on ready ears for one reason: we religious don't want to challenge the status quo because, despite our protestations to the contrary, we benefit from it, and these benefits have numbed us to the injustice being perpetrated by the hierarchical systems that act as though they have been divinely instituted.

By the time I presented my reflections — whose core ideas are now contained in this book — it had become clearer to me that we religious are too cavalier when we proclaim ourselves a "prophetic voice" in our culture and church. We have not really probed deeply what it would mean to be prophetic today in light of the Scriptures. Thus my effort in this book is to present the challenge that lies ahead for all religious if we are truly called to be a prophetic presence in our church and world. While my reflections apply to all religious throughout the world, they will specifically address the reality of being a religious brother who lives as a priest in the Roman Church as a citizen of that nation which is the world's most powerful political economy.

The following chapters will examine (1) the theological and sociological role of prophecy in the Old Testament; (2) the relationship among charism, prophecy, control, and institutionalization as Jesus and our founders saw these issues; (3) what Isaiah, Jeremiah, and Ezekiel, the three "major prophets," can teach us about authentic holiness; and (4) what following this prophetic call demands of us, specifically how non-assent and non-submission might work to challenge the world of politics, economics, and church.

The question of how religious life is prophetic has arisen not just from our own self-reflection as religious; indeed it also constitutes the dominant image used for religious in key documents arising from recent official institutional teaching about the role of religious today. Yet I hope to show that the prophetic character of religious life faces inherent opposition that could undermine the possibility of being prophetic, and I will contend that this opposition comes not only from external sources — the institutional church and political economy — but from internal dynamics as well, insofar as we have a significant number of our own members who have never really embraced their prophetic call because they joined religious life with another understanding of its purpose.

Given this dilemma, I have found it useful to examine the historical and cultural dynamics that gave rise to prophecy, especially the three "major prophets," to garner from them what we religious must do to become prophets in the biblical sense. Isaiah, Jeremiah, and Ezekiel offer us a compelling and enduring witness of the charism of prophecy as it must be exercised by us religious today. Isaiah 1–39 provides for us the basis for the mystical/prophetic call itself. Jeremiah shows us the need to become "people of the scroll" who can allow the Word to become incarnate in our lives in ways that may lead to persecution. Ezekiel-in-Exile stands as a model of how to criticize the current reality of a political economy and a clericalized church while remaining energized to create alternative communities grounded in authentic contemplation, justice, and solidarity with others who have been marginalized.

The final chapter will offer my thoughts on non-assent and non-submission and how these principled stances of nonviolent resistance to injustice could be manifested in the wider society as well as the institutional church. The book will conclude with criteria that might be used to determine whether and how religious might embrace the prophetic demand to disagree and non-comply with current teaching or practice in the empire as well as the official church when the situation seems to merit it.

The Problem of Official Church Teaching about Religious Life as "Prophetic"

When I entered the Midwest Province of the Capuchin Franciscans, the idea of religious life as prophetic was not even imagined beyond telling ourselves that wearing a beard, habit, and sandals was "countercultural." Indeed I accepted both church and society on their own terms. For me, and for almost everyone else entering religious life, it was important to reach the highest state of perfection. Thus it was unimaginable that I join the Third Order Regulars; I needed to be part of the First Order. And among the First Order, I believed the Capuchin Franciscans witnessed to a higher form of Franciscan life than the other Franciscans called "Observants" and "Conventuals."

And then came Vatican II. In its core document on the church it highlighted the centrality of baptism as the equalizer for all, as well as the "universal call to holiness" or perfection. In the same document, *Lumen Gentium,* it abandoned "state of perfection" language; rather it called us to live the Gospel through the embrace of the evangelical counsels. Commenting on this changed way of thinking about religious life, Patricia Walter notes: "Religious life, then, is clearly of divine, not ecclesiastical, origin: it is a gift in and to the church."[2] If this is so it must be reflected in the way we live the evangelical counsels — including obedience, which is always made to God primarily and then, secondarily, within the church.

While *Perfectae Caritatis* (Decree on the Appropriate Renewal of the Religious Life) was a conciliar attempt to flesh out the implications about religious life contained in *Lumen Gentium,* it was Pope Paul VI's *Evangelica Testificatio* (Apostolic Exhortation on the Renewal of the Religious Life

According to the Teaching of the Second Vatican Council, 1971) that truly situated religious life in the context of the universal call to holiness. In so doing, according to Walter, it "is a landmark in official theology of religious life."[3] Far from identifying religious life as a function under the authority of the institutional church, it was highlighted as a "concrete sign" and "privileged witness" of a constant search for the Absolute and one's total commitment to the inauguration of God's reign. The vows exist to bring about the good news of God's reign, especially among the poor. Consequently the vows can no longer be limited to ascetical practices; they are critiques of specific forms of social sin. While this makes the vows, according to Walter, "a prophetic sign rather than as a means of escaping historical reality or simply as pointers to some heavenly future,"[4] the word "prophet" is still missing from the document when it characterizes the identity of religious in the contemporary world.

In 1978 *Mutuae Relationes* (Directives for the Mutual Relations between Bishops and Religious in the Church, from the Congregation for Religious and for Secular Institutes, and the Congregation for Bishops) discussed the relationships religious were to have with bishops. Building on *Lumen Gentium* and *Evangelica Testificatio*, the document stressed the role of the Holy Spirit as the underpinning of religious life. Noting that the charism of the founders represents "an experience of the Spirit," this pneumatic grounding of the charism of religious life was to serve as the first responsibility of superiors. Thus fidelity to the charism historically precedes fidelity to the magisterium; indeed it is the role of the official church to safeguard that uniquely charismatic character.[5]

The official identification of religious with the prophetic role would not find any significant mention until 1978, in "Religious Life and Human Promotion." Here we find religious life defined as "charismatic and prophetic"[6] insofar as it witnesses to a new way of living communally in anticipation of God's trinitarian reign and challenges the world to do the same.

Not much further was noted about religious being "prophetic" until the 1994 Ninth Ordinary General Assembly of the Synod of Bishops. It met to discuss the topic "The Consecrated Life and Its Mission in the Church and in the World." Before they met, many religious, like myself, were asked to respond to a working document that had been distributed, but as the synod evolved, and especially after its deliberations, it became clear that our voices concerning religious life as prophetic were not about to be heard.

Some might challenge this assessment: How can I say that religious have not been listened to on this issue when, at the synod itself, a key element discussed by the Fathers was the prophetic dimension of religious life? How can I believe that our vision of religious life as prophetic was not heard when, after the synod, Pope John Paul II stressed this very element in his apostolic constitution on the synod, *Vita Consecrata?* Indeed, a major section of this document was titled "A Prophetic Witness in the Face of Great Challenges," in which, the pope said, there is "a prophetic dimension which belongs to the consecrated life as such, resulting from the radical nature of the following of Christ and of the subsequent dedication to the mission characteristic of the consecrated life." How can I question whether we religious can be truly prophetic when the pope himself declares: "The sign value, which the Second Vatican Council acknowledges in the consecrated life, is expressed in prophetic witness to the primacy which God and the truths of the Gospel have in the Christian Life"?[7]

The basis for my assessment comes upon further and closer reading. The pope acknowledges that in the history of the church "there have been men and women consecrated to God who, through a special gift of the Holy Spirit, have carried out a genuinely prophetic ministry, speaking in the name of God to all, even to the pastors of the Church." He quotes Vatican II's Dogmatic Constitution on the Church as saying the Holy Spirit "furnishes and directs her [the Church] with various gifts, both hierarchical and charismatic."[8] But then he states unequivocally that this "prophetic stimulus" can be "guaranteed" only when it functions in "full harmony with the Church's Magisterium and discipline."

While the Vatican Council said the Spirit's gifts were "both hierarchical and charismatic," Pope John Paul II's emphasis makes clear that any charismatic dimension of the church, such as that found in the prophetic character of religious life, will never serve as a check or balance to any (ab)use of power in the priestly group, as it did in the Old Testament. Rather it is the other way around: religious life — prophetic or otherwise — must always come under the authority of the clerical group in order to be in "full harmony with the Church's Magisterium and discipline." In subsuming the prophetic function within and under the institutional (i.e., priestly or clerical) function, the pope and the clerical hierarchy create a contradiction and vitiate any possibility of a true prophetic challenge to their power. This subordination was then further reinforced in CICLSAL's June 14, 2002 instruction on consecrated life in the third millennium.[9] Such a clericalized approach to the prophetic also reinforces a major Protestant concern about the way the Roman Catholic Church bureaucracy has evolved; Paul Tillich described it well when he pointed to its canonically constituted authoritarian structure with its "exclusion of . . . prophetic criticism."[10]

The Problem of Religious Accepting Religious Life as "Prophetic"

Now official, institutional church teaching has defined religious life as essentially prophetic. Following the recommendations of the Second Vatican Council, religious embraced the mandate to "read the signs of the times and return to the gospel according to the charism of their founders." Faithful to this conciliar directive, we began to reinterpret our lives as revolving around the poles of prophecy and contemplation, with solidarity with the poor and marginalized and commitment to social justice as the benchmarks of the authentic expression of these two poles in our lives. While we always had stressed the need for contemplation, the prophetic dimension became more explicit in our self-understanding as individuals, groups, and congregations. Thus Sister Kathleen Pruitt, past president of the U.S. Leadership Conference of Women Religious (LCWR), reiterated this critical dimension when she said in her 2002 address at LCWR: "Religious life in its very essence is prophetic. And so, it would seem that our congregations . . . are called to claim and to live into the dynamic tension of the call to be prophetic — to be prophets of hope."[11]

That we religious have defined ourselves as "prophetic" has thus been the case for at least a generation. As I reflected on the process by which we came to define and accept ourselves as such, I realized I had been at some important gatherings that helped forge our understanding of ourselves as prophetic.

Almost two decades ago I was a speaker at a grassroots effort of religious who were gathered to "read the signs of the times" in a way that would help us create an identity and direction for our future. Called "Convergence," the meeting convened hundreds of religious in Chicago, Los

Angeles, and Springfield, Massachusetts. In all three venues the results of the groups' discernment highlighted the twin poles of prophecy and contemplation as our core characteristics. In fact, we realized that the one cannot be understood apart from the other, if we are to be rooted in solid biblical soil. Authentic prophecy, biblically speaking, flows from the mystical experience; the mystical experience is empty without its proclamation in prophecy. As feminist biblical scholar and I.H.M. sister Sandra Schneiders has said: "Prophetic action is the public face of mysticism."[12]

The "Convergence" conclusions regarding the contemporary character of religious was replicated almost perfectly in 1989 when the Leadership Conference of Women Religious and the Conference of Major Superiors of Men (CMSM) met jointly in Louisville, an assembly in which I participated. We gathered to envision what we called the "transformative elements for religious life in the future," and we agreed that the foundation of religious life flowed from its two core elements. If we are to be transformed individually, communally, and congregationally as religious in our church and wider world, this transformation needs to be grounded in a "prophetic witness" and a "contemplative attitude toward life." In explicating what we mean by becoming "prophetic witnesses in church and society," we said: "Being converted by the example of Jesus and the values of the gospel, religious life in the year 2010 will serve a prophetic role in church and society. Living this prophetic witness will include critiquing societal and ecclesial values and structure[s], calling for systemic change and being converted by the marginalized with whom we serve." Regarding the second element that should characterize our future as religious, we highlighted our need to witness to what we call a "contemplative attitude toward life." We declared: "Religious in 2010 will have a contemplative attitude toward all creation. They will be attentive to and motivated by the presence of the sacred in their own inner journeys, in the lives of others, and throughout creation. Recognizing contemplation as a way of life for the whole church they will see themselves and their communities as centers of spirituality and the experience of God."[13]

Around the same time, Vincentian priest David Nygren and Sister of St. Joseph of Carondolet Miriam Ukeritis began what became an extensive study of religious in the United States. The "Religious Life Futures Project" involved a national survey of 816 religious congregations and some 126,000 individual religious. Besides responding to the initial questionnaire, I was one of the religious chosen to be part of the "Visioning Group," which met in Colorado. The theoretical basis for the study revolved around the notion of "transformation": As the authors noted in their 1992 final executive summary of their findings, they used the term "transformation" organizationally insofar as it "refers basically to qualitative discontinuous shifts in organizational members' shared understandings of the organization, accompanied by changes in the organization's mission, strategy, and formal and informal structures."[14]

The authors noted that transformation usually begins with a crisis that reveals the fact that "the organization's current shared understandings are no longer adequate." In reaction to this, the "easiest response for the organization to take" is denial: it will defend itself and, perhaps, not address the data at all. The life-giving response is to "'unfreeze' organizational members' present understandings of the organization by presenting a significant challenge to their validity."[15]

Authentic prophecy flows from the mystical experience; the mystical experience is empty without its proclamation in prophecy.

When the survey asked questions regarding prophetic behavior, such as identifying with the poor, calling for social or systemic change, and religious sensing themselves as countercultural or alienated from the dominant consciousness and culture, the data showed a stark contrast between the way we articulate our lives as "prophetic" and our everyday behaviors. Members showed little commitment to working with the poor and little connection between their personal and spiritual fulfillment and working for systemic change.[16] The data also showed that religious have become assimilated into the dominant culture, are often unaware of the degree of their assimilation but yet "agree that to remain distinctive in the world, this trend toward assimilation must be reversed."[17]

When the Nygren-Ukeritis study was released, I was a member of the Justice and Peace Committee of the Major Superiors of Men. This took me to the headquarters of LCWR and CMSM in Silver Spring, Maryland. There I found echoed what I had heard from other religious all around the country as I traveled: there was bias in the study; it was skewed from the beginning; the methodology was wrong. The consequence? Not only did religious take what the authors had predicted would be the "easiest response for the organization to take," namely, defensiveness and denial, but to this day I know of no religious congregation or organization of religious congregations that has taken seriously the challenges of the findings. Yet we continue to call ourselves prophetic and countercultural.

What is the problem in putting this vision into practice? Why might some religious act very prophetically but in ways often isolated from and even rejected by the wider membership?

That we religious have come to perceive our life to be prophetic is not limited to notions developed in the United States. This became quite clear to me in 1993 when I participated in a meeting of religious from around the world in Manila. We gathered, having read the signs of the times in our own settings, and as we convened, we asked if we found any commonalities that would enable us to act in greater solidarity. Again, the prophetic dimension of religious life rose to the top of the mix. Realizing that "the theology shaping our hearts, our minds, and our souls as well as our thoughts, passion, and action cannot be anything but prophetic," we stated that such a "prophecy will not properly exercise its role until it challenges both priest and king — the cleric and the culture — from the perspective of the poor and the demands for social justice."[18]

Given the statements made in the Synod on Religious Life, the writings of Pope John Paul II in *Vita Consecrata* and CICLSAL itself, to say nothing of those self-definitions made by us religious ourselves whether here or in places like our gathering in Manila, at the grassroots or highest levels, I believe strongly that the prophetic dimension must characterize us religious if we are to contribute anything unique to the church and wider world, if we are to provide a check and a balance to the actions of "priests" and "kings." Why then do we seem to be falling so short of the mark? What is the problem in putting this vision into practice? Why might some religious act very prophetically but in ways often isolated from and even rejected by the wider membership? Why have our formation programs failed to prepare adequately for a kind of life in this society and church that would be considered "prophetic"? Just as my own province submitted to Rome's unilateral decision not to accept our election of a lay brother as provincial, why are so many religious communities and congregations so muted? Rather than simply continuing to call ourselves "prophetic," I think we need to embark upon a reality check that brings us back to earth.

The Difficulty of Putting into Practice Proclamations about Religious as Prophetic

In her monumental study on religious life, Sandra Schneiders makes it clear that the prophetic dimension of religious life will find members of religious congregations acting "prophetically" in different ways, given their various social locations. She writes:

> Every form of Religious Life is called to be prophetic in a situation that cannot be generalized to or deduced from some archetypal and abstract context. American Religious at the turn of the twenty-first century, even in a context of galloping globalization, cannot be equated with African Religious in a rural village or Asian Religious in a Hindu culture. Solidarity with the people among whom one lives involves one in a specific cultural setting with its specific issues.[19]

Given this nuanced view, we must consider the many ways individual religious are being prophetic vis-à-vis the "culture of death" that defines our Western way of life. We find evidence in their presence at right-to-life rallies and protests at the School of the Americas. We also find them at shareholder meetings and demonstrations challenging the negative forms of globalization. Some are arrested and go to jail, even for long periods (witness the three Grand Rapids Dominicans). However, when it comes to a *corporate* presence in the institutional church, we find few if any religious congregations *publicly* and *regularly* challenging the abuse of patriarchal power — whether these abuses be related to ordination concerns or to issues of various rights within the church. When it comes to entire groups of religious acting prophetically, our witness wanes in power and visibility. Too often, the vision of religious as prophetic remains just that: a vision, an ideal, words on paper rather than a witness made public.

The dichotomy has been well-described by the Erie (Pennsylvania) Benedictine Joan Chittister. A member of a religious community widely praised for the unique way it nonviolently resisted the Vatican, she writes:

> In the name of the spiritual life we go to bed early and ignore the poor; we get up early to pray and forget the exhausted; we live in our warm convents and forget the people in the tenements; we tell ourselves that we are too old, too young, too small, too insignificant to do the things we used to do and so we give ourselves permission to cease to be a presence, a prophetic voice. And we call it religious life. And we wonder why it's dying.[20]

Another voice challenging the ways we religious define ourselves as prophetic comes from another religious whom I consider, as an individual, to be "prophetic," Richard Rohr. Referring to the minister general of his Franciscan order, who said Franciscans "are more curious than significant," Rohr said in 2002 that "religious life has been totally co-opted." Speaking about new recruits in congregations of men like his and mine, he stated: "They like us, but they don't tend to take us seriously. In my opinion, they know that they can often live a life more on the edge outside of religious life. We are not liminal anymore, we are just a stop on the pony express." Then, moving to a critique of our structures he declared: "Corporately, we are totally co-opted, part of the system, enjoying its benefits too much to critique or confront either church or society."[21]

Rohr's comments about our entrenchment in the clerical church and consumer culture remind me of a passage from Morris West's 1963 novel, *The Shoes of the Fisherman*. Pope Kiril (modeled on Pope John XXIII) is talking to the paleontologist Telemon (modeled on Pierre Teilhard de Chardin) about the situation of the world and religion in particular. Bemoaning the fact that so few witness to the need for a radical transformation of church and society, he muses:

A man like St. Francis of Assisi, for instance. What does he really mean?... A complete break with the pattern of history.... A man born out of due time. A sudden, unexplained revival of the primitive spirit of Christianity. The work he began still continues.... But it is not the same. The revolution is over. The revolutionaries have become conformists. The little brothers of the Little Poor Man are rattling alms boxes in the railway square or dealing in real estate to the profit of the order.... Of course, that isn't the whole story. They teach, they preach, they do the work of God as best they know, but it is no longer a revolution.[22]

The fictional pope's insight about the way the charism of our founders has become "routinized" has haunted me ever since I first read Kiril's conclusion: "The revolutionaries have become conformists."

Though I will later show how such conformity evolved with the clericalization of our church and its overarching influence in our congregations, we now cannot see our conundrum and crisis apart from the context in which we are called to be prophetic. And society itself presents another challenge to our witnessing to our founders' original prophetic visions. One can wonder whether a truly prophetic style of life can even be imagined, much less lived.

I first came to wonder if this might not be the case when I read a passage from Saul Alinsky, the great community organizer. In his 1971 "bible" on the subject, *Rules for Radicals*, he writes:

The *New York Times* some years ago reported the case of a man who converted to Catholicism at around the age of forty and then, filled with the zeal of a convert, determined to emulate as far as possible the life of St. Francis of Assisi. He withdrew his life's savings, about $2,300. He took this money out in $5 bills. Armed with his bundle of $5 bills, he went down to the poorest section of New York City, the Bowery (this was before the time of urban renewal), and every time a needy-looking man or woman passed by him he would step up and say, "Please take this...." Our friend attempting to live a Christian life and emulate St. Francis of Assisi found that he could do so for only forty minutes before being arrested by a Christian police officer, driven to Bellevue Hospital by a Christian ambulance doctor, and pronounced non compos mentis by a

Christian psychiatrist. Christianity is beyond the experience of a Christian-professing-but-not-practicing population.[23]

Especially in a culture like ours in the United States, if "Christianity is beyond the experience of a Christian-professing-but-not-practicing population" and if "the revolutionaries have become conformists," again, I think we need to ask ourselves: Are we being honest when we religious call ourselves "prophetic"? Would it not be more authentic to stop calling ourselves prophetic and let others do so if they see us acting in a prophetic way? Wouldn't it be better if we just do the best we can in the manner that has sustained us comfortably in our current lifestyle? Furthermore, is it even possible for us to create prophetic *communities* and not end up being manipulated or muted rather than maligned and manhandled, as Jesus promised those who would be faithful (see Matt. 5:10–16; 10:16–23)?

In the Hebrew Scripture we find a kind of checks-and-balances approach to the way Israel would be governed. It envisioned unique and separate, albeit related and interconnected, roles of priest, prophet, and ruler. One of the Second Vatican Council's documents on the church, *Lumen Gentium*, built on this triad when it showed how all the baptized are fully part of the People of God insofar as the commonality among bishops, priests, and laity resides in the threefold forms of Jesus' ministry of priest, prophet, and ruler.[24] Because it stressed religious life to be more a way of life than a ministry, the Council did not apply the triad to religious.

Given the dynamics of a clericalized church that demands that all charisms identified with the prophetic function come under the authority of the priestly function, as well as the dynamics of the increasingly imperial ways of the U.S. government, which effectively has established hegemony over the world itself, I find it very sad that, at the very time the prophetic function is so sorely needed, the *"ekklēsía"* and "empire" have undermined its raison d'être, with barely a protest from us. Despite this bulwark of opposition, I am not ready to capitulate in face of these almost insurmountable forces that have become buttressed by an ideology of selective state supremacy and papal infallibility. At the same time, however, I am no longer willing to support talk about religious being "prophetic" if we cannot produce the fruits of prophecy beyond this or that individual, communal, or periodic corporate action. There must be something institutional that *constitutes and sustains ourselves in the prophetic tradition.* Such a task challenges us to link any prophetic call/charism with a deeper probe of what prophecy meant in the past in a way that will nourish and nurture us in the future. The present book is intended to provide the biblical and theological ground for such a prophetic constitution.

In recent books on religious life that have discussed its prophetic character[25] almost none have a significant grounding in those biblical forerunners called "prophets," whose followers gathered around them in "prophetic" enclaves (i.e., schools or communities). Even though David Flemming, Gerald Arbuckle, et al. stress the need for the prophetic witness of "refounding" individuals, their approach to "rebirth through conversion" places the stress on individuals rather than groups, to say nothing of the supposed "prophetic" constitution of religious life itself. For her part, Schneiders develops the prophetic dimension of religious life and stresses its function for the church more than society,[26] but she does not develop her ideas from the prophets themselves. Similarly, although the title of my book may evoke Diarmuid O'Murchu's *Religious Life: A Prophetic Vision: Hope and Promise for Tomorrow*,[27] our books differ significantly. O'Murchu's book is "prophetic" insofar as it outlines a futuristic dream of what religious life might become. While such futuristic envisioning might be "prophetic" insofar as it is future-oriented and thus addresses a definite need, I believe we religious need to probe the historical context that gave rise to the phenomenon of the biblical prophets and challenge ourselves from there.

One

An Overview of Prophecy in Scripture and Tradition

The Rise of Prophetic Voices in Israel/Judah's History

From Israel's earliest times prophets were part of its lifeblood. God gave Abraham the name "prophet" (Gen. 20:7). Exodus speaks of Aaron (Exod. 7:1) and Miriam, his sister, as prophets (Exod. 15:20). However, Deuteronomy tells us, their brother Moses stood beyond them in prophetic stature: "Never . . . has there arisen a prophet in Israel like Moses, whom the Lord knew face to face. He was unequaled for all the signs and wonders that the Lord sent him to perform in the land of Egypt, against Pharaoh and all his servants and his entire land, and for all the mighty deeds and all the terrifying displays of power that Moses performed in the sight of all Israel" (Deut. 34:10–12).

While patriarchs like Moses were regarded as prophets because of their divine calling, with the rise of the kings we find "royal prophets." They existed at the behest of the ruling powers. Given their court appointment, their persons as well as their prophecy could easily be co-opted by the kings. But not always, as we know from the story of how the prophet Nathan challenged David. David had coveted, violated, and impregnated Bathsheba, the daughter of Eliam and wife of Uriah the Hittite (2 Sam. 11:2–5). To cover it up, he assigned Uriah to a place where he could easily be killed. When this happened and "the mourning was over, David sent and brought her [Bathsheba] to his house, and she became his wife, and bore him a son" (2 Sam. 11:27). This ploy "displeased the Lord, and the Lord sent Nathan to David" (2 Sam. 12:1–2).

Nathan told David a parable about a rich man and a poor man and how the rich man exploited the poor man. "Then David's anger was greatly kindled against the man. He said to Nathan, 'As the Lord lives, the man

23

who has done this deserves to die'" (2 Sam. 12:5). At that, "Nathan said to David, 'You are the man'" (2 Sam. 12:7). Rather than attacking the messenger who exposed his duplicity, David admitted his sin. Later, tradition holds, he composed the famous Psalm 51. It begins with the words:

> Have mercy on me, O God, according to your steadfast love;
> according to your abundant mercy blot out my transgressions.
> Wash me thoroughly from my iniquity, and cleanse me from my sin.
> For I know my transgressions, and my sin is ever before me.
> Against you, you alone, have I sinned, and done what is evil in your
>   sight,
> so that you are justified in your sentence and blameless when you
>   pass judgment.
> Indeed, I was born guilty, a sinner when my mother conceived me.
>   (Ps. 51:1–5)

David was succeeded by Solomon, the son born to him of Bathsheba. With King Solomon's death in 922[1] Israel was divided into a Northern Kingdom, "Israel," with Samaria as its capital, and a Southern Kingdom, "Judah," with its capital in Jerusalem. Prophets roamed in both places. Some were false prophets, others were true.

The Old Testament speaks about prophets like Deborah (Jud. 4:4) and Samuel (1 Sam. 3:20; 9:9), along with priests and rulers, who were part and parcel of the landscape of Israel/Judah's geography of faith.[2] Ahijah and Jehu were prophets who spoke to the leaders of the Northern Kingdom, as did Elijah and Elisha. However, with Amos and Hosea we find the beginning of unique kinds of "prophets." They seemed divinely inspired and are recognized as such by having books in the Scriptures named after them and their prophecies. These are the classical prophets. They have been defined so not because they have been chosen to discern God's will through human appointment but because they were inspired directly by God to tell humans, especially human leaders of the court and the cult, that their modes of operating did not correspond to God's ways. These charismatic prophets functioned by divine command, not human fiat. Because they spoke against human aberrations, they often were persecuted and killed by those in the court and cult who were threatened by their prophecies.

In the Southern Kingdom, the prophecy of Isaiah found in chapters 1–39 (First Isaiah) took place "in the days of Uzziah, Jotham, Ahaz, and Hezekiah, kings of Judah" (i.e., 742–701). Micah also prophesied during this period. In 722 Israel fell to the Assyrians under King Sargon; twenty-seven years later Judah almost capitulated. No specific names of prophets during the reigns of Manasseh and Amon are noted in the Scriptures; however, the Second Book of Kings makes it clear not only that Manasseh's whole reign of fifty-five years involved "evil in the sight of the Lord" (2 Kings 21:2–9) but that God's prophets chastised him (2 Kings 21:10). Amon, his son, ruled only two years but continued the evil ways of his father. No mention of prophets speaking against him can be found. He was succeeded by his son Josiah (2 Kings 21:26).

Jeremiah's prophecy covered the period (628–582) of Kings Josiah (in the thirteenth year of his reign), Jehoiakim, and "until the end of the eleventh year of King Zedekiah son of Josiah of Judah, until the captivity of Jerusalem in the fifth month" (Jer. 1:1–3). In 605 BCE, the Chaldeans defeated the Egyptians under the leadership of the famous King Nebuchadnezzar. With this victory Babylon became the region's dominant military force. At that time Josiah ruled Judah (2 Kings 22:1). He had a brother, Prince Zedekiah. Josiah's successor was his son Jehoiakim. He tried to play off the Egyptians and Babylonians but lost when the Babylonians got the upper hand in 598. When he died shortly after, his eighteen-year-old son, Jehoiakim, replaced him. Three months after Jehoiakim became king, in 597, the Chaldeans under Nebuchadnezzar attacked Jerusalem and Judah. Jehoiakim surrendered and was taken to Babylon, eight hundred miles away. With him went the nation's aristocracy, including the priest we know as the prophet Ezekiel. Jehoiakim's uncle, Zedekiah, was installed by Nebuchadnezzar as his puppet in Judea.

Under Zedekiah life continued in much the same way until 587. At that time Babylon discovered its puppet "king," Zedekiah, was planning an alliance with the Egyptians (against Jeremiah's warning). So it laid siege and occupied Jerusalem (2 Kings 25:18–21; Jer. 52:15ff). This second defeat was devastating. Now all but the poorest people and necessary artisans were exiled to Babylon. The year this occurred, 587–586, has become known as the Exile's official date; it was devastating for priests, prophets, and people. In Tamara Eskenazi's words: "The trauma was not only physical, though it was first of all that. It was also psychological and spiritual, since destruction and exile undermined everything the survivors held secure and trustworthy. A stunned people wrestled with the meaning of their experience. Many no doubt simply gave up; they died in despair or blended in with the surrounding peoples. Some, however, turned to the prophets for explanation and direction."[3] One of them whom we will consider in this book was Ezekiel. His whole prophecy took place during this exile.

In 539, Babylon fell to the Persian forces of Cyrus. Because he was quite benevolent and actually urged the Jews to return to Jerusalem to restore the temple (2 Chron. 36:23; Ezra:1:1–4; 5:13–17; 6:3–5) Cyrus was given the titles "shepherd" (Isa. 44:28) and God's "anointed" (Isa. 45:1).

The Identity and Message of Prophets in the Old Testament

As we try to determine whether a voice identified as "prophetic" can be considered authentic, we need to understand that the Hebrew Scriptures contain at least four different words for "prophet."

The first kind of prophets that Jews recognized as such were "diviners," individuals who received specific information from God, which they, in turn, communicated to God's people. The Hebrew word for such a person is *rōeh*, or "seer," because these prophets had the power to penetrate secrets of the heart and/or foretell the future.

A second category of prophet in the Jewish tradition is one who experiences a heavenly vision. Such a "seer" was often called a mystic, a [c]rōeh. The classic example of such a prophet or visionary is Isaiah; we will examine his vision in the next chapter.

The third type of prophet in the Hebrew Scriptures is the most common, the *nâbî*, one who has been called and commissioned with a message, and it is from *prophētēs*, the Greek translation of *nâbî* (or *nebî*), that we get our word "prophet": one "who speaks on behalf of another." They spoke on behalf of God (Exod. 7:1); they served as God's spokesperson. True prophets knew theirs to be an authentic call from God based on their experience (Amos 7:14–16; Isa. 6:1–13; Jer. 28:15–17). But the only way others could tell the difference between true prophets and false prophets rested on their prophecy's future fulfillment; only "time will tell." Consequently there would be many false prophets, as God said through

Jeremiah: "I did not send the prophets, yet they ran; I did not speak to them, yet they prophesied" (Jer. 23:21).

While the *nâbî* did speak about the future, their main preoccupation covered the present life of their people and the culture that sustained them. Their concern addressed the current situation as they had come to critique it from their experience of divine inspiration; their words spoke to the aberrations in their world that alienated the people from God's concerns.

To ensure the continuation of their message, given their realization of societal resistance to embracing it, some prophets created communities around them, and in these enclaves disciples would be schooled in the vision experienced and proclaimed by the prophet. Consequently, two entities became the objects of the prophets' preoccupation: the wider society whose mores would be challenged and the alternative community of their followers they needed to nurture into being. In this latter situation, the prophetic call of the individual was extended into a community by the Spirit. "This suggests," Joseph Blenkinsopp writes: "that their inspiration, while being a gift of the Spirit to them as persons, is given because of the community to which they belong and is tied up somehow with their community of consciousness."[4] The disciples of the *nâbî*, the *nâbî-im*, felt called by God to continue proclaiming the message of their leaders: to reveal God's concerns to their contemporaries.

The fourth kind of prophet is the one so defined by others. Thus the Samaritan woman in John's Gospel used the term of Jesus (John 4:19). Such a person is recognized as holy or sent by God. In Hebrew they were called *îha'elōhîm*. They were believed to have received special blessings from God and stood among the people as a witness to God's holiness.

In many ways for religious today, the diversity of prophetic types is an important element of our tradition to appreciate. In this effort, I find most helpful the work of the Jewish author Abraham J. Heschel. His two-volume work, *The Prophets*, is a classic. Just a quick review of some of the sectional titles provides us with an even wider sense of prophecy: a prophet is an assayer, messenger, witness, at one with God and God's people, wrathful against indifference, an iconoclast, inspired by the demand for justice, intimately related, understanding God as having pathos in an apathetic world, one having cosmic sympathy.

In *The Prophets II* Heschel devotes a whole chapter to the interplay among "prophet, priest, and king." In the wider world beyond Israel and Judah, some nations divinized their rulers, but unlike these nations, the Jews never considered their king to be divine, only divinely anointed. Furthermore, the king's anointing was balanced by another divine anointing: that given the priests. When some kings tried to arrogate to themselves the prerogatives of the priestly anointing, the priests were quick to challenge them, as when King Uzziah was excoriated by the priest for trying to burn incense before the altar (2 Chron. 26:16ff).

While the rulers and the priests had different divinely appointed functions, as did the court-appointed prophets, the classical prophets operated as a third force in Israel and Judah. Divinely inspired, they served as a kind of check and balance to any abuse of power exercised by the rulers, the priests, or the court-appointed prophets. An example of this, according to Heschel, can be found in the way that "mercilessly Jeremiah condemned the kings, the princes, the priests, and the *nebiim*" (2:26; 4:9; 8:1; 13:13; 32:32; cf. 14:18; 29:1).[5]

Building on this extensive and complex history of prophecy in Jewish tradition, Christian author Walter Brueggemann applies the concept of prophecy to our contemporary society and church. A key insight of Brueggemann, drawn from his 1978 classic, *The Prophetic Imagination,* is what he calls "the task of prophetic ministry." He insists prophetic ministry must "nurture, nourish, and evoke a consciousness and perception alternative to the consciousness and perception of the dominant culture around us."

In his explanation of what he means by "prophetic consciousness," Brueggemann begins with the prophetic vision of Moses. He then describes how Moses translated his call and commission into a viable message to enable his people to make their exodus. Next, in turning to Solomon, Brueggemann finds one who "was able to counter completely the counter-culture of Moses."[6] His Solomon had to unravel and confront the interplay of economics, politics, and religion. He challenged his dominant culture by his prophetic ministry; he also offered his adherents an alternative consciousness and community to match.

When we examine the cultural mindset that sustains the prevailing economics of affluence today there don't seem to be that many religious witnessing either God's pathos or God's wrath regarding the shadow side of globalization and its injustice. As Alan Wolfe has written of the wider population, we religious have become much like the majority in our nation who simply "do not care about income inequality."[7] When it comes to the politics of oppression, too few of us seem genuinely concerned that the leaders of our country talk about democracy quite selectively as they support regimes that actively suppress it — when this is "in our strategic interest." On the home front, we find efforts at campaign finance reform being consistently undermined. When we consider how, with globalization, the politics of oppression sustains us few in the economics of affluence, we also can see how easily our "good life" increasingly can be realized only at the expense of planetary integrity. With our larger houses having almost every creature comfort and in almost every shape and size, it's hard to deny how deeply the dominant consciousness has captured our corporate souls.

As we read the daily papers that expose the secret and subtle ways many leaders representing the institutional dimension of our Catholic religion (in which a "god" exists whose power can be immanent or present only in a system defined by their clerical control) the virtual silence of the religious bodies of women and men is sad indeed. As the clerics have created an apparatus accountable to none beyond themselves and sanctioned it with a male god to support its patriarchal culture, our voices are muzzled in fear at exposing its bankruptcy. For instance, during the Boston scandal of 2002–3, even as lay people mobilized themselves into the Voice of the Faithful and scores of priests organized to protest the abuse of their ordinary's power, religious congregations of men and women seemed noticeably absent.

If the Boston experience might be considered premonitory, the fact that the lay people (i.e., the ruling group) as well as many clerics (i.e., the priestly group) came to a newly found "prophetic consciousness" exposes the limited understanding we religious have about prophecy when we identify it exclusively with a periodic letter written to a congressperson, an annual filing of a shareholder resolution, or picketing for women's rights at a cathedral on the day of priestly ordination. As important as these witnesses may be, as they are expressed, it is equally important not to overlook the deeper political, economic, and religious sin that needs to be unmasked. For Brueggemann, prophetic ministry has to do not primarily with addressing specific public crises but with addressing, in season and out of season, the dominant crisis that is enduring and resilient, of having our alternative vocation co-opted and domesticated. It may be, of course, that this enduring crisis manifests itself in any given time around concrete issues, but it concerns the enduring crisis [for instance, the links among the military and industrial system sustaining our political economy which finds the "official church" virtually silent] that runs from concrete issue to concrete issue.

Brueggemann's interpretation of prophetic ministry nurtures a consciousness that is an alternative to the dominant way of thinking or ideology that pervades one's environment. This alternative vision contains a negative as well as positive function; as it denounces the sinful situation it announces a hope-filled future and the creation of an alternative community of resistance. While it "serves to criticize in dismantling the dominant consciousness," it also "serves to energize persons and communities by its promise of another time and situation toward which the community of faith may move."[8] While it says "no," its alternative "yes" envisions a way out of the morass.

Second, as noted in the way both priests and laity organized in Boston, it's important to realize that the unilateral abuse of power by a small group can be challenged only by the creative and nonviolent use of power by those who organize against it. This demands the creation of communities of resistance that sustain the individual and corporate acts of prophecy. Brueggemann has shown that in order to ensure that the prophetic ministry will not die with the persecution or death of the prophet at the hands of those threatened in the political economy or religion, there developed what he calls a "natural habitat" for such prophetic voices: alternative communities of consciousness. These subcommunities stand in tension with the dominant community; this represents their denunciatory role. At the same time, they witness to another way of exercising power in mutuality and collaboration.

In *Religious Life: A Prophetic Vision*, O'Murchu calls such subcommunities "liminal." Building on the original notion applied to Benedictines by Richard Endres, O'Murchu says they offer "an ambiguous, sacred, social state in which a person or group of persons is separated for a time from the normal structures of society. . . . Every society has a structure, and a liminal community both clarifies the structure of society and can be instrumental in changing it."[9] This notion of religious life as "liminal" has subsequently been promoted by almost all those writing on the subject.

The history of the prophets, which reveals their ministry as criticizing and energizing on the one hand, while creating alternative, liminal communities on the other, brings our reflections on the history of the prophetic movement to another level: a deeper examination of the role of a charismatic founder and how the sociological notion of charism relates to biblical prophecy.

Charism and Prophecy in Scripture and Tradition

In a 1997 book, *Prophecy and Prophets*, edited by Yehoshua Gitay, all the chapters except one narrate details about the person and message of various prophets in the Old Testament. The exception, "Max Weber, Charisma and Biblical Prophecy," by Ronald E. Clements, shows how *sociologists* rather than biblicists have helped us understand and interpret the phenomenon of prophecy and the role of the prophet. Clements examines what sociology can teach us about the evolution of prophecy and obstacles to it in the Old Testament.

Building on Weber's insights, Clements interprets the Old Testament prophets as charismatic figures. He shows clearly how the original charism stimulated the prophetic founder to challenge society:

> That prophecy was vitally important as a medium through which Israel and Judah could interpret, and come to terms with, these tragic events [the misfortunes of the Davidic dynasty and the Jerusalem temple] lies in the very nature of charismatic authority. The prophet's claim to be able to speak directly on behalf of God placed him outside the more traditional and rational forms of authority of ongoing religious institutions. He felt no compulsion to submit to them, and did not need to appeal to them for his legitimacy.[10]

In time, the charism gradually is co-opted as those schooled in the ways of the prophet are co-opted by or adapt to the wider society. Weber calls this process of enculturation the "routinization of the charism." When this institutionalization takes over, the followers pay lip-service to the founder; their lives, however, show they have been seduced by the dominant culture.

Max Weber's insights into the rise and routinization of religious movements are helpful in understanding how mainline religious life has atrophied in the West. As I have applied his insights to provinces like my own, I find a consistent pattern expressed over and over.[11] In summary, the process of foundation begins when the current religious patterns in a society no longer give life — at least to the individual who is revealed as possessing the charism. The routinization or institutionalization of a previous religious vision evokes in some woman or man anomie, or mean-inglessness. Inspired by an alternative vision, the person not only begins to articulate or profess his or her values and ideals but puts them into practice via an alternative mode of living through fresh and life-giving norms and traditions. Thus the "limit situation" of meaninglessness invites liminality or a meaning that differentiates one from the previous malaise. When the profession (orthodoxy) of the values and ideals coincide with a practice in viable norms and traditions (orthopraxy) a religious movement reaches its apogee.

However, once the founder or charismatic figure dies or loses influence, invariably those who followed that person find something missing. They often continue to go through the motions of a life that once had meaning for them until gradually the institutionalized dynamics, with their norms and traditions in the name of the values and ideals that seem further and further removed from the lived reality of the members, come to dominate. This "routinization of the charism" of the founder results in a kind of mechanization. When this occurs, the maintenance of the institution and the interests of its increasingly controlling priests (i.e., "clerics") becomes more important than the original mission and vision of the founder.

Institutional preservation is ensured through appeals to norms and tra-ditions, rubrics and rituals that sustain the power of the ruling clericalized group. With this, alienation or anomie among the rank and file begins. This mechanical approach to the original vision and the need to maintain the monuments rather than ensure the vision make the situation ripe for the rise of another charismatic figure to offer an alternative way of life. With the decay of the former model, a new model must emerge if the prophetic vision is to be sustained.

Weber's pattern describing the rise of the charismatic founder (the "prophet") in response to societal anomie and the routinization of the prophet's charism seems to apply to almost every religious movement. In particular this model makes sense of the emergence of Jesus' own prophetic ministry within the context of an overly clericalized Jewish religion and Roman imperial domination.

The Jesus Movement

When Jesus began preaching and working wonders (Luke 3:23–5:9) in a prophetic way (Luke 4:17ff) his vision stood as an alternative to the prevailing imperial and religious modes of operating. It attracted others to join him (Luke 5:10–11), and in good Jewish prophetic tradition, his fledgling movement became an observable community around him. His way of life set him and them apart from the wider society, while also threatening the existing institutions, with resulting persecution. With his death and resurrection, the inspirited Jesus movement (as noted in the Acts of the Apostles) grew rapidly, and for two and a half centuries it was constituted as a semi-egalitarian group with priests and bishops accountable to the laity. All members were perceived as having their own unique gifts, which were necessary for the full functioning of the ecclesial body.

Key among the gifts was prophecy. Indeed, in Paul's listing the core charisms of the church, the gift of prophecy "is the only constant and it is always given second place, sometimes to the office of apostle, otherwise only to the gift of love (1 Cor. 12:8–11, 28–30; 13:1–2; Rom. 12:6–8)....The authentic prophet gives an intelligible message and functions always to build up the church."[12] With its dynamism ensured by a healthy interaction and an interplay among the various gifts, the early ecclesial organization of the Jesus movement also thrived because of persecution from forces outside the group before its original charismatic thrust was institutionalized and clericalized with Constantine's declaration of Christianity as the official religion of the Roman empire. Recalling the original inspiration — when the Spirit's charisms rather than male clericalism defined the early church, Medical Mission sister Miriam Therese Winter writes:

In the room where the Pentecost presence of God blew the lid off traditional ways of exclusion and strict, hierarchical control, a chaotic tangle of new beginnings and unlimited potential was instigated by the Spirit. Everyone responded according to the Spirit, who led each in turn from within. Juxtapose this image with the more recent one of eleven elderly men sequestered together in a room in Rome, cut off from the rest of the body of Christ, secretly deciding how the Church will proceed, afraid to let go of the way we were as a result of centuries of accretion, afraid to hear the Spirit speaking words that lack prior approval, afraid to throw open the doors of the heart to allow love's Pentecostal fire to purge and transform us all. Surely this can't be what God had in mind for the Church of the twenty-first century.[13]

While this complete subversion of Jesus' original vision of God's reign in the power of the inclusive Spirit was not at all what Jesus intended, the Jesus movement becoming imperial Christianity occurred as the natural evolution of all religious institutions.

This Constantinianization of the church mirrors sociologically what happened when Israel left behind its days of persecution and came out of the desert. Almost immediately, the Scriptures tell us, Israel's institutionalization of religion (Jer. 2:7–8; 22:21) gave rise to the need for prophetic voices to challenge the monumentalization process (see Jer. 2:9–13). Unfortunately for Israel — as with the Christians once they left the catacombs — prophetic voices speaking against such bureaucratization will not be heard. Thus Jeremiah declared of the hardness of heart in his own religious institution: "From the day that your ancestors came out of the land of Egypt until this day, I have persistently sent all my servants the prophets to them, day after day; yet they did not listen to me, or pay attention, but they stiffened their necks. They did worse than their ancestors did" (Jer. 7:25–26).

When this routinization of the original charism occurred within Christianity, alienation and anomie took over, Christianity became Christendom, and what had been a prophetic movement became mechanized. In the process the male, ever more clericalized and clericalizing group now in power took on the patterns of authority based not on the evangelical way of Jesus (Matt. 20:25–26) but on an imperial and pharisaical model of authority. What was normal in the political and religious culture of the time soon became normative in the church, and before long the normative was enshrined in canons and laws. Thus, an authoritarian, hierarchical process that deviated from the more egalitarian structuring of power manifested in the words and deeds of a prophetic, anti-establishment Jesus became defined as divinely inspired, divinely willed, and divinely sanctioned. Not surprisingly, people felt alienated and longed for a return to the original gospel vision. The result? According to Jerome Murphy-O'Connor, "It is not without significance that religious communities began to be formed at precisely the moment that Christianity became the official religion of the empire." He explains:

> With the establishment of Christianity, membership in the despised sect was seen to have definite advantage, and whole cities and countries became Chrisitian. The Church became a social institution, and bureaucracy and ceremony conspired to push the element of true community into the background. It was then that certain individuals began to see the difference between the Church as they knew it and the first Christian communities, and to recreate deliberately the ideal described in the Acts of the Apostles (Acts 2:44–47; 4:32–35).[14]

Eventually this phenomenon of institutionalization gave rise to new charismatic men like Benedict and Bernard and movements like Benedictinism and the Cistercians. When their charisms in turn were routinized, new movements arose. While the early Franciscan movement was characterized by an egalitarian and democratic thrust, its evolution found its own clericalization and institutionalization.

Whether Israel's history that gave rise to the need for prophets, or the creation of religious movements in the face of the Constantinian Roman Church, or the need for a contemporary return to the prophetic call in religious congregations, a sociological understanding of how charisms become clericalized enables us to better examine the problems we face in the current situation of the Roman Catholic Church.

The Charisms of Prophecy and Authority in the Roman Church

Before the Gospels were written in their present form, in his First Letter to the Corinthians Paul wrote that the members of that church "are the body of Christ and individually members of it. And God has appointed in the church first apostles, second prophets, third teachers" (1 Cor. 12:27–28a). In other words, the apostolic function, the prophetic function, and the teaching function originally were envisioned as three separate ministries authorized by God for the proper ordering of the church. Then Paul goes on to add other charisms given the church by God: "then deeds of power, then gifts of healing, forms of assistance, forms of leadership, [and] various kinds of tongues" (1 Cor. 12:28b). While the apostolic charism took priority over other "forms of leadership," it was not to be exercised without recognizing the role of other forms of power in the church. When it actually came to leadership or the use of the power in the church, there had to be balance.

From the beginning, balance based on the primacy of Jesus, as the Christ of the community, characterizes Paul's early letters. Addressing the inherited social, economic, and religious mores of the converts of his time, Paul stressed the need for individuals to be respected in the communities as well as local churches and to see themselves as part of the whole. In the process he outlined a way of living in the churches that opposed the prevailing culture while struggling to overcome those forces that continually impinged on the new alternative way of living "in Christ."

Writing a few decades later, in the only Gospel to use the word for "church" (*ekklēsía*), Matthew stressed the need for two power poles in the *ekklēsía*, both able to bind and loose. This God-ordained pattern was to be the norm for an effective and evangelical way of using the power to bind and loose in the church. The first would be that identified with Peter as the head of the community of disciples to whom would be given the keys (Matt. 16:16–20); the second would be grounded at the local level, in the disciples themselves who would be promised the abiding presence of Jesus in their midst (Matt. 18:17–20).

The word *ekklēsía*, or "church," occurs only three times in all four Gospels; all three are found in these two passages of Matthew. Unfortunately Catholics have been taught about only the first form of power in the church. As such this part of the Catholic tradition has proven itself just as fundamentalistic as any non-Catholic tradition that stresses one scriptural text to the exclusion of others. The two texts read:

The "Church of Matthew 16"

[17]Blessed are you, Simon son of Jonah! For flesh and blood has not revealed this to you, but my Father in heaven. [18]And I tell you, you are Peter, and on this rock I will build my church and the gates of Hades will not prevail against it. [19]I will give you the keys of the kingdom of heaven, and whatever you bind on earth will be bound in heaven, and whatever you loose on earth will be loosed in heaven. (Matt. 16:16–19)

The "Church of Matthew 18"

[17] If the member refuses to listen to them, tell it to the church; and if the offender refuses to listen even to the church, let such a one be to you as a Gentile and a tax collector. [18]Truly I tell you, whatever you bind on earth will be bound in heaven, and whatever you loose on earth will be loosed in heaven. [19]Again, truly I tell you, if two of you agree on earth about anything you ask, it will be done for you by my Father in heaven. [20]For where two or three are gathered in my name, I am there among them. (Matt. 18:17–20)

The text from Matthew 16 represents an insertion placed by the Matthean editor of words not found in the accounts of Mark and Luke. Mark and Luke also have Simon Peter declaring Jesus to be "the Christ," but without any special commendation from Jesus for so doing. For our tradition to place such a great stress on the Matthean insertion when Mark, his source, and Luke do not contain it invites the critique of fundamentalism made by the Pontifical Biblical Commission: "In what concerns the Gospels, fundamentalism does not take into account the development of the Gospel tradition, but naively confuses the final stage of this tradition (what the evangelists have written) with the initial (the words and deeds of the historical Jesus)."[15] As I understand the commission's words and put the text in its historical context, it would seem Jesus himself never even pronounced these words. If not, should the passage not be interpreted in a more nuanced manner? Should we have created such a patriarchal and clerical organization around this text, especially when it may never have been a dominical saying? While it certainly is part of the canonical text and therefore part of our faith, should it be so pivotal? Should our whole faith as Catholics de facto be so bound by this passage? Should the claims to the church's patriarchal clericalism be bound by this text when its context and Matthew 18 invite a more balanced and inclusive approach to authority and decision making in the Church?

What I call the Petrine "Church of Matthew 16" (or what Rahner called the "Church of officialdom"[16]) must be balanced with the collegial "Church of Matthew 18." To do otherwise not only reveals a clerical bias; it also serves to justify the unilateral abuse of power and further dysfunction in the body of the church as a whole. When imbalance like this takes over in the church, Cardinal Walter Kasper has said, you not only have dysfunction; it is "close to heresy. You cannot make a unilateral system of our faith, because our faith is aimed at a mystery, and in mystery there are different aspects and approaches." In effect, he emphasizes: "No one has the whole truth; that is only found together."[17]

While the power identified with the keys in the "Church of Matthew 16" represents a definite and unique form of authority not given the "Church of Matthew 18," neither can this power be exercised isolated or independent of the other power to bind and lose grounded in the "Church of Matthew 18," which is promised the presence and confirmation of Jesus Christ when its power is exercised (Matt. 18:18–20). Today our church needs prophets to remind the priestly group who abuse the text in order to ensure their clerical power that power in the church cannot be based on just one text if other texts contribute to a fuller understanding of how that power should be exercised. If the one "church" is isolated from the other we will have only an apostolic church without a complementary church of disciples. To have this clericalized "church" as the sole determinant of the validity of any prophetic utterance will further undermine the integrity of the body as a whole. For this reason the church needs prophets to remind its priests that Matthew 16 cannot be divorced from Matthew 18 and Matthew itself cannot be divorced from the other Synoptics, John, Paul, or the other Scriptures.

If people insist on remaining only with Matthew 16, however, I would suggest that we read a bit further than the three verses that Matthew added. We see that the very first utterance upon Peter's reception of "the keys" brought forth a stinging rebuke from Jesus. "From that time on," Jesus "began to show his disciples that he must go to Jerusalem and undergo great suffering at the hands of the elders and chief priests and scribes, and be killed, and on the third day be raised," Matthew tells us. And then we are told Peter "took him aside and began to rebuke him, saying, 'God forbid it, Lord! This must never happen to you'" (Matt. 16:21–22). At that, Jesus "turned and said to Peter, 'Get behind me, Satan! You are a stumbling block to me; for you are setting your mind not on divine things" but on man-made ways of thinking (Matt. 16:23). I find it of interest that few remember this passage, which immediately follows the words which we believe constitute Peter and his successors as teaching infallibly when they speak "from the chair." The text shows that Peter was not only wrong in his first pronouncement upon receiving the "keys"; Jesus declared that his words did not represent God's divine way of thinking. On the contrary, it represented a way of thinking that limited God's vision to one *man's* interpretation. Despite Peter's proclamation, which he backed up by invoking God's authority, this first pronouncement of the "first pope" was far from infallible; indeed, it was totally rejected by Jesus himself.

An unbiased interpretation of the texts concerning authority and the power to "bind and loose" in the church simply demands more nuance than the current clericalized and ideological interpretation. Having gone beyond its New Testament authority, the males constituting the church of Matthew 16 teach the members of the church of Matthew 18 that there exists only one source possessing divine authority: the male, clerical class of Matthew 16. Buttressed by its own clerically originated and clerically defined norms and traditions, it claims that it alone holds full authority or jurisdiction — from and through the top down — in the person and office of the pope (including the Curia, or what we call the papacy), the bishops (the episcopacy), and the priests (the rectory). In its most negative manifestation, its male-only, clerical members see themselves as the sole determinants of what is God's will. Nothing is acknowledged as divinely inspired except what they interpret to be so through their clerical fiat. At the local level it is expressed as "Father will/won't ..."; at the diocesan level it revolves around orders from the chancery; at the highest level all authority resides in Rome. With such male, clericalized control, prophecy loses its voice.

In his apostolic exhortation on religious life (*Vita Consecrata,* 1996) John Paul II acknowledges the traditional functions of priest, prophet, and ruler, but declares that anything "prophetic" must be recognized as such by the priestly group: the hierarchy and papacy. Any individual or collective prophetic voices will be considered authentic only if these are sanctioned by the priestly class. The effect of such teaching is simple: the prophetic voice will always be subsumed under the self-perpetuating patriarchal, clerical control of the priests.

This need for maintenance over mission became clear at the Second Vatican Council. There Cardinal Leo Suenens suggested that the document on the church (*Lumen Gentium*) note how all the baptized share in Christ's prophetic office. Cardinal Ernesto Ruffini prevailed on behalf of the traditionalists when he argued that any emphasis on the charisms of the Spirit in the church could endanger the prerogatives of those in the institutional church.[18] Tradition trumped the Scriptures; clericalization triumphed over the charisms.

In a speech entitled "Do Not Stifle the Spirit," Karl Rahner said that God's Spirit can never be limited to what he called the church's "official" life, its principles, sacramental system, and teaching. But, in effect, this is what has happened. The "official" church has evolved to a point where its charismatic element has been crushed. Rahner called this routinization of the founding charism of Jesus Christ "a situation dominated by a spirit which has been rather too hasty and too uncompromising in taking the dogmatic definition of the primacy of the pope in the Church as the bond of unity and the guarantee of truth." He noted that this dogmatization had been interpreted to justify "a not inconsiderable degree of centralization of government in an ecclesiastical bureaucracy at Rome."[19]

Authentic prophecy must ultimately be grounded in the power of God's Spirit. The legitimacy of its claims must arise, not from the power of the priests, but from the power of God's intervening word over all those faulty and half-truthful interpretations of God's word that profane the integrity of that word. When such clericalization of the prophetic character of the church occurs, God's word itself can be nullified for the sake of a tradition.

This obsession of the leaders in our tradition to maintain their control can be seen in the example of the Oblates of Mary Immaculate in their dealings with the Vatican. In writing their constitutions to reflect the spirit of the Second Vatican Council, the OMIs read the signs of the times and returned to the Scriptures that they might reinterpret their charism for contemporary life. They considered how the model of Mary, whom Catholic tradition reveres as "Regina Prophetarum," might serve as their human inspiration. Referencing her own understanding of how the world would be transformed through her instrumentality, they wrote a passage in their constitutions that contained the following statement based on the Magnificat of Luke's Gospel:

We are members of the prophetic Church. While recognizing our own need for conversion, we bear witness to God's holiness and justice. We announce the liberating presence of Jesus Christ and the new world born in his resurrection. We will hear and make heard the clamour of the voiceless, which is a cry to God who brings down the mighty from their thrones and exalts the lowly (cf. Luke 1:52).

When they submitted their constitutions for approval, SCRIS (as CICLSAL was called then) told them to remove the passage cited from Luke. When they resisted, asking why they should remove the scriptural reference, SCRIS told them the statement was too radical and inflammatory. When the OMIs held their ground, insisting that they were including a divinely inspired scriptural passage that might serve as a model for their Marian imitation, SCRIS agreed that they could include the text only if they immediately followed the reference with these words: "This prophetic mission is carried out in communion with the church, in conformity with the directives of the hierarchy and in dependence on our Superiors."[20] In the case of the OMIs even divine inspiration must be controlled by curial fiat!

When we religious hear stories like this, or face conflicts with the Vatican regarding the contemporary application of our own charisms (such as electing nonordained brothers for full leadership), it's natural to conclude things are amiss; something is just not right. Rather than quickly trying to find a rationale for the Vatican, much less offering an apologia for such abuse, our intuitions and conclusions should not be discounted too quickly. Indeed they may be promptings of the Holy Spirit inviting us in the depths of our consciences to proclaim another vision rather than to have our vision obscured or our mouths silenced. In such a situation (lest I be considered disloyal for advocating such a form of authentic obedience instead of simple submission) I have been helped immeasurably by further insights on the matter of charism vs. clericalism offered by Karl Rahner.

Aware of the tendency of the clerical leaders to abrogate power unto themselves, Rahner taught that the charismatic dimension of the church actually takes priority over the institutional element. He regarded "the institutional element in the Church simply as one of the regulating factors (albeit a necessary one)"[21] for the charisms. For him jurisdictional power in the institutional church is secondary or "encompassed by the charismatic movement of the Spirit in the Church, the Spirit who again and again ushers the Church as an open system into a future which God alone and no one else has arranged."[22] In other words, the Spirit's direct exercise of power precedes any other expression of power in the body of Christ as it is organized in human forms.

Building on Rahner, John Haughey argues that until the "Constantini-anization of the church" in the fourth century great significance was placed on the role of the gifts of the Spirit in the church. Divinely bestowed for the common good, these charisms, in fact, created the church's very identity and ensured its ministerial manifestations. However, in 411, in a sure sign of the routinization of the charism of the founder, Pope Innocent I went so far as to decree that only bishops could invoke the Holy Spirit. While this decree might have been objectively heretical, bureaucratically it attempted to put the process of bringing the Holy Spirit into the church under the effective control of the human authority of the papacy and bishops. The priority of the human over the divine was inverted.[23] The system started suffocating its very life-source; divine inspiration became the servant of human decisions.

Eight centuries later, at a high point in the bureaucratization of the church, Francis of Assisi envisioned a healthy balance between authority in the order arising from canonical jurisdiction and his understanding of the Holy Spirit giving the gifts equally to all solemnly professed members, including those in leadership. Thomas of Celano tells us that "With God," Francis said, "there is no respect of persons, and the minister general of the order, the Holy Spirit, rests equally upon the poor and the simple." Francis wanted this thought inserted into his rule, but since it was already approved by papal bull, this could not be done.[24] Francis sought to found his order upon the deepest authority he could imagine: the Holy Spirit who knows no such distinctions among persons.

Addressing Some Internal Obstacles That Keep Religious from Being Prophetic

In 1986 I was one of two delegates from North America to the Fifth Plenary Council of my Capuchin Franciscan order. Held in the State of Rio Grande de Sol, Brazil, its theme was "Our Prophetic Presence in the World." I had attended meetings in Rome previous to the Brazil meeting to prepare for the month-long gathering. On the basis of my participation in the preparatory as well as plenary meetings, I concluded it would be better if we Capuchins stopped referring to ourselves as prophetic. I also wondered why we, as representatives of the whole order, were devoting ourselves to being "prophets" when we never had been corporately persecuted for justice' sake — as were "prophets before" us (see Matt. 5:11–12).

When I returned to the United States my task was to convey the vision of the Fifth Plenary Council and its document "Our Prophetic Presence in the World" to the superiors (ministers provincial) of the North American provinces. Despite my concerns about calling ourselves "prophetic," I came to their meeting excited about my mandate from the Plenary Council. After all, what other regional group in the world represented such an opportunity to implement the order's vision than we who lived in two of our world's most powerful nations? Sad to say, once I shared the council's vision and goals, one provincial minister effectively scuttled a North American implementation of the vision from Brazil. He was opposed to framing Capuchin Franciscan life in terms of a prophetic dimension that would revolve around justice, peace, and the integrity of creation, and his opposition was not effectively challenged by the other leaders. It wasn't that they were against it; it was that they were not themselves convinced about its being critical to our future. The vision died; to this day the Capuchins in Canada and the United States have never worked together to implement a "prophetic presence in the world." None of these men were ill-willed. But they were ill-prepared theologically and charismatically to be the kind of leaders that the document would demand. Sadly, in the United States and Canada, as a result Capuchin Franciscan life, I believe, has been less effective.

I think it safe to say that their reluctance to embrace this way of linking religious life and prophecy is representative of many who entered our way of life before the Second Vatican Council. Could it be that they never fully embraced the renewal that the council envisioned? They entered with one set of assumptions about religious life, believing themselves called to minister in institutions that were part and parcel of what it meant then to be "Catholic." This Catholicism was clerical and triumphal. They now were being called to witness to a servant kind of presence that would put them in solidarity with the poor and require them to challenge a system that enriched the wealthy at the expense of the poor. Committed as they are, they want to support their groups' direction toward greater solidarity with the poor. However, in research conducted since 1978, David Couturier, a fellow Capuchin, has continually found that fully 60–80 percent of religious men and women, despite their sincerely held and publicly proclaimed commitment to the poor, are fundamentally ambivalent with regard to the reality of the plight of the poor.[25] Is it any wonder that some might resist the new direction? Furthermore, is it any wonder why communities are conflicted when data also shows that over 50 percent of the youngest men and almost 75 percent of the youngest women in religious life have noted that it has been "important" or "very important" as religious to work with the poor?[26]

Couturier has been a pioneer in addressing the need for those entering the formation programs of religious congregations to be involved in structural conversion; he is one of the few. Despite his efforts, I have not yet seen fruits that indicate new initiates in formation have, corporately, challenged the "system."

Entering with One Set of Values; Finding Ourselves Needing to Practice Others

People like me who entered religious life before the Vatican Council entered at the apogee of its institutional and bureaucratic phase. I recall bragging about our province's newly built seminary in Crown Point, Indiana. It was not only the largest Capuchin building in the world; it housed more Capuchin students than any other "monastery" (not "friary," as we now call our houses) in the world.

Religious life at that time was in its prime. If we saw ourselves as countercultural institutionally it was because of the alternative educational, health care, and service ministries we created. We built institutions and assigned individuals to staff them in such large numbers that lay people were never even considered necessary for their functioning (unless these institutions were hospitals). Those entering novitiates learned about the canonical demands related to religious life rather than the charismatic gifts. Law dominated Spirit. Formation prepared initiates for apostolic activity in a hierarchical and clerical church that went unquestioned and uncritiqued.

Rarely did we leave the seminary. If we did, it would be to visit doctors (when they could not come to us). We were self-enclosed and self-contained. Our buildings housed tailor shops, bakeries, cobbler shops, barber shops — everything to enable us to exist apart from the wider world. When we would leave these buildings to exercise our apostolates, we were told to return home as quickly as possible lest "regular life" be tarnished or we be contaminated by the ways of the world. We were to be in the world — within our own institutions as far as possible — but never of the world. Joan Chittister describes this "world" well:

> For centuries religious commitment implied a degree of disinterest in the affairs of the world in which [religious] lived. Dualism, the war between the spiritual and material dimensions of life, cast suspicion over anything not directly related to the spiritual life. Jansenism, the theological rationale for making withdrawal itself the spiritual hall-mark of the religious lifestyle, rooted religious life in a rigid lifestyle far outside the flow of new life patterns in an urban, industrial society. By the nineteenth century, the deed was done: Religious life had become a culture within a culture.[27]

In my own Midwest Province, we were so institutionalized and regularized that the exact daily schedule was followed throughout its territory. This applied equally to over four hundred men from Detroit to Montana. All of us rose at 4:55 a.m. to say prescribed prayers and Mass in Latin. We all wore the same type of habit; we ate and recreated together at the same time. Such legislated practices fit us into the sociological description of a "total institution," which Erving Goffman described so well — with prisons being the prime example.[28] Like inmates in civilian prisons we too followed rigid rules, were divided between guards and inmates (superiors and subjects), changed our names upon entrance, and wore a mandated uniform at all times. Submission to rules and regulations enacted by others defined our lives. Unlike civilian prisoners, we never questioned the pattern. We accepted our status and embraced it as part of God's will for us. Deviation from this "norm" resulted in exclusion.

The social upheavals of the 1960s and the religious revival inaugurated by the Second Vatican Council had their effect on our religious congregations. Desire for change among the rank and file religious chafing under such rigidity was originally opposed by most superiors. They believed it was their duty to preserve the system they had inherited. To their surprise, their appeals to obedience, accompanied by resistance to any change, resulted in even greater dissent and demands for "adaptation" and "renewal."

Meanwhile, "in the world" now used to resistance to rigid authority structures from government to universities, mainline Catholics, benefiting from their Catholic institutions and watching their incomes equal if not exceed those of their non-Catholic peers, started to reflect the values of those in the wider culture and its institutions. With traditional Catholic institutions no longer needed to make it "in the world," religious would no longer be needed to provide their traditional work force. The very raison d'être that once motivated scores of young people to fill novitiates was no longer relevant. An entirely new understanding of what it would mean to be a dedicated Catholic in "the world" was sweeping old patterns away. Joan Chittister explains:

> Slowly but surely they began to leave the Catholic enclaves which had sheltered and sequestered them from public harm, to insert themselves with confidence into the wider population, to go to public hospitals and to send their children to public colleges. Slowly and steadily they blended into the culture around them in almost everything except churchgoing. To be Catholic became a religion rather than a way of life.[29]

In the mid-1960s, when adaptation of the rigid norms and traditions finally came, its purpose was not that we might become prophetic but that we might get rid of centuries-old accretions that made us "irrelevant" in "the world." The old norms and traditions institutionalized over scores of years had as their goal the elimination of any uniqueness among us. Now, in our effort to show our relevance to the world, we uncritically accepted its values and mores, especially its individualism. Given our desire to "make it" in the world, any prophetic stance against its consciousness and culture came not from religious but from popes like John XXIII and Paul VI, who challenged Catholics to embrace the church's social teachings. However, for Catholics who had already succumbed to the dominant culture of consumer capitalism any prophetic words of popes about economic injustice would evoke a response like that of William Buckley: "*Mater Si, Magistra No.*" The institutional church might be mother to the faithful, but its teachings were no longer useful for understanding our political economy, much less how it might be oppressing people and the planet. That the imperial consciousness had come to dominate the moral grounding of many Catholics became abundantly clear in 2003 when three main Catholic neoconservative writers (John Neuhaus, Michael Novak, and George Weigel) all put forward rationales as to why the papal position against going to war with Iraq could be disobeyed in good conscience.[30]

My province enacted changes in our lifestyle in 1966. At the "Adaptation Chapter" the delegates agreed to drop a uniform hour plan, changed the habit by making the beard optional (for us Capuchins the beard had been part of the habit), excised the daily litany to Mary and prayers invoking the Capuchin saints. They said other devotions were optional. Soon, however, it became clear that just changing traditions and time-honored customs was not enough for our renewal. Because our charism had become identified with such norms and rituals to the point that they had come to give us our very identity, the changes evoked deeper questions about our raison d'être. This found us asking: *In whom or what do we believe? What are our underlying values and ideals? What is our message to the world? Who are we?* We really didn't know!

We had never studied the charism of Francis and Clare; we examined only the canonical demands and obligations connected with nonobservance of the Rule. If any of us probed Franciscanism more deeper, we did so in study groups outside the daily regimen or curriculum. Unfortunately, when our "Values Chapter" did take place in 1969, our deliberations were not grounded in a reading of the "signs of the times" and a consequent "return to the Gospel" as prescribed by the Vatican Council. Consequently, our "appropriate renewal of religious life" around the charism took place isolated from both the culture and the gospel. We mimetically took from European "experts" their latest studies on Francis and the Franciscan values of poverty, minority, fraternity and disponibility (a word from outside our Anglo-Saxon linguistic tradition, meaning availability). Because these values did not arise from a felt need or personal or communal experience, they were never embraced in ways that would invite accountability for their implementation and, therefore, a new kind of obedience. To this day, at least among us Capuchins in the United States and English-speaking Canada, they have never been accepted enough to be invoked as a unifying force that might invite us to a renewed corporate kind of presence in church and society.

This brief overview reveals, in my mind, one of the biggest obstacles facing our members as we now are being told our life as religious is to be prophetic: our fundamental calling to witness to the charism of prophecy has never been collectively embraced as a result of truly understanding the world in which it must be witnessed and the Scriptures upon which it is to be based. If our members have never sufficiently embraced the notion of being "prophetic," it is little wonder that efforts to promote the prophetic dimension of religious life face resistance or defiance. However, until this issue is honestly addressed in a way that will give it individual, communal, and collective expression, I believe we in the mainline religious congregations will continue to experience diminishment and even death.

The research conducted in 1993 of Canadian women religious by Notre Dame sister Janet Malone further demonstrates my contention that we have not embraced the call to be prophetic in the Roman Church. In a 2001 article, "Prophets in Religious Life," she tells how respondents were given the statement: "I think our prophets are/are not accepted (circle one) in my congregation because...." She did not define "prophet," because she wanted people to answer from their own understanding of the term. Despite the "understanding that unless they accepted the prophetic stance, their congregations would die," forty-five of the eighty-five respondents said the prophets were not accepted, thirty-four thought they were accepted, and six were unsure or did not know.[31]

Studies of new candidates for religious life attest to the same conclusion: not only is the "prophetic" dimension of religious life far from their "radar screen," they are ambivalent even about identifying with the victims of the social sins of church and society. Indeed, while young religious express high values regarding their willingness to sacrifice for others, at the same time they have demonstrated significant trends for aggression, domination of others, and avoidance of harm and criticism.[32] Dean Hoge confirmed this trend of the last twenty years toward social conformism and escapism among those in formation in male, clerical groups in 2003.[33] Is it any wonder new recruits are reluctant to challenge any sin in the "empire" except that of abortion, much less any sin in the church itself? Indeed, they find themselves willingly embracing the church's forms of control and quite willing to promote them.

As helpful as Janet Malone's research is, I believe asking why religious are not prophetic is disingenuous if we do not face the fact that many religious entered religious life not to be prophetic but to be accommodationist. As a result I believe Malone herself skirts the real issue when she asks why "many congregations seem to have had their prophetic edge dulled." She ponders:

> Is it because of blindness and denial of the rather "obvious" signs of the times? An inward focus on survival? Ongoing but ineffective attempts (religious globalization?) to truly restructure? Forays into renewing foundering ministries with people too old and worn out? Futile efforts to replenish diminishing ranks in a model of religious life that is gone? Collusion with a consumeristic, big-business society deluged with advertising-slick vocational promotion on the Internet and billboards, complete with freebies such as website "addresses" and . . . key chains, pens, and holy cards? Ongoing confusion between common life and community life?
>
> Do such questions point to the extent to which religious life has moved away from its prophetic raison d'être as counterculture, in which it upholds and lives out, in sacred trust, those values and ideals for which all yearn?[34]

A radical restructuring of religious life is needed. I concur with Malone when she concludes: "At this point in the life cycle of our congregations, in the midst of our chaos, it is time to refound, not renew. All our well-intentioned renewal efforts have focused on 'cosmetic' changes; only refounding deals with the core issue of religious life, the prophetic."[35]

Some might argue that, because of their embrace of celibacy, religious are prophetic in relation to a sex-obsessed world. While this notion may have some merit, few seem to be joining religious life, at least in the "North," precisely because it has been unable to offer a solid evangelical reason why celibacy must be at its core. In developing nations, thousands are willing to accept celibacy in order to become religious, but one can ask why the prophetic character is so lacking even there. Indian Jesuit Kurien Kunnumpuram comments: "On the face of it, Religious Life is flourishing in our country. There are close to one hundred thousand Religious in India today. But how many of them are prepared to be prophets of the Lord and pay the price for it? There are no reliable data available. It is my impression that only a minority of Religious is radically committed to the following of Christ."[36]

As I noted in the introduction, only a few contemporary writers on religious life have probed what it means to be prophetic, and even these efforts have been limited and sporadic. In his *Religious Life: A Prophetic Vision*, O'Murchu does not talk about religious life as "prophetic" in terms of biblical prophecy but as related to a new way of living in the future. One who comes close to writing about religious life in terms of biblical prophecy is Gerald Arbuckle. Yet even in his *Out of Chaos: Refounding Religious Congregations*, he never examines what the implications regarding biblical prophecy might be for contemporary religious. Nor does he talk about the need for new communities to become the context for refounding groups. Though he does ground his findings in the sociology of Max Weber, he does not seem to understand the radical reform needed *within religious life* that demands such a renewal of mind and restructuring of purpose and direction. He limits the notion of "prophetic" to "refounding" individuals.

If our members have never sufficiently accepted the idea of being "prophetic," it is little wonder that efforts to promote the prophetic dimension of religious life face resistance or defiance.

When I talk on the charism of religious life, I usually examine the phenomenon of religious movements and chart their institutionalization. I show that historically, sociologically (à la Weber), and anthropologically (à la Wallace),[37] no religious group that has been institutionalized into the "monument" phase has been able to transform itself. While I have observed such "conversion" occur in some corporations because they faced serious loss of market share, I have not found parallels in any religious institution. This is perhaps because denial keeps the members from comprehending the cultural causes of the group's diminishment. Or possibly delusion makes us believe our erosion can be reversed simply by saying more prayers for vocations and avoiding a fundamental rethinking of religious life. In face of such resistance, and because I do not think a critical mass within the institution can now be formed to address this task, I believe that what is needed is the creation of a alternative religious groups within the existing institutions.

The main opposition to such alternative communities is that these might undermine the integrity of the community. But what integrity? The peace that seems to prevail at the expense of prophecy? Jesus himself was unable to transform his own Jewish institution and from the beginning created his own *nâbîim*, or "house of disciples." Yet I face continual resistance from the leadership as well as many rank and file religious when I call for such alternative communities. For a case in point, in 2002, years after the call for us Franciscans to become prophetic, one group of Third Order Franciscans rejected my contention that we need small alternative communities. They honestly believed they would be able to transform themselves institutionally as well as communally and personally. They would not accept my arguments or the conclusions of such studies as those of Nygren and Ukeritis that the group dynamics and mindset of their congregation would not allow the transformation to take place. As their numbers continue to decrease, they refuse to offer corporate support to those members who want to start something new in a more prophetic vein.

Another concern I have with Malone, despite her valuable insights regarding the need to refound existing religious congregations, is that she seems to have fallen into the trap of thinking, with Gerald Arbuckle,[38] that "some" in religious life might be "called" to the prophetic life and that prophecy may not be the call for all of us. These "some" she calls the "ugly ducklings"; they must learn to swim and survive in unwelcoming waters. That she acknowledges that the wider community has made such prophets its ugly ducklings attests to how far the wider community has failed to be renewed. If religious life itself is a call to be prophetic, all those called to religious life must be prophetic; there can be no exceptions for this or that person, much less this or that community or congregation.

If our underlying charism is constitutively prophetic, I would ask whether those who joined religious life under other assumptions might be fully justified in leaving our congregations if they are not able to live our "new" charism authentically. The Catholic culture that was the context for religious life for those born before the end of the Second World War is not the context in which religious life must be lived today. Simply

put, the religious life that we entered then will never be the same. As Joan
Chittister writes:

> The world that spawned religious life, even the religious life of this
> century [the twentieth], is not the world we're living in. If religious
> life has anything to do with real life, the hope of recasting it in old
> molds smacks of pure fantasy. Spending time and energy yearning
> for the return of the mythical past while the present swirls perilously
> around us, awash in the debris of rationalism in the social order and
> dogmatism in the church, only holds us back.[39]

The Dominant Consciousness of Individualism and Its Effect on Community

In their groundbreaking analysis of the U.S. culture, Robert Bellah and
his fellow researchers showed that as a people we have moved from being
identified personally by our membership in the communities of which we
are a part into an individualism that interprets the whole as existing to
meet our needs. We have moved historically from being a people identified with biblical and republican values to an individualism defined by
self-interest. "Instead of directing cultural and individual energies toward
relating the self to its larger context," Bellah and his co-authors wrote,
"the culture . . . urges a strenuous effort to make of our particular segment
of life a small world of its own."[40] If the wider society fits our particular
segment of life, we will incorporate it; if not, it will not be our concern.
The consequence is a breakdown of commitment to any group beyond
one's immediate self-interest. Thus "community" becomes secondary to
the "individual."

With the increasing globalization of the U.S.-dominated media and
economy, the cultural values of individualism are being effectively ex-
ported and embraced throughout the world. Instead of standing as a
prophetic challenge to this individualism through the creation of alternative forms of authentic community, too often we religious have been
critically compromised. "Religious, like most other humans," Barbara
Fiand writes, "are culturally affected much more than we are countercultural."[41] Furthermore, as the Nygren-Ukeritis study of religious life has
shown, we are often "unaware of the degree" of our "assimilation into the

mainstream culture and how invisible" we have "become to those who would most call out" to us.[42] Consequently, any attempts to address the corrosion of community that has resulted — at the very time new recruits come to us from this culture wanting to find new ways of experiencing community — are undermined, challenged, or dismissed as irrelevant.

In the document "Our Prophetic Presence in the World," created at the meeting of the Capuchin Franciscan order in Brazil in 1986, we examined the phenomenon of individualism as it was affecting our fraternities and undermining their integrity not only in the developed nations but in the fast-growing developing world as well. As we shared our experiences it soon became apparent that the kinds of individualism Bellah and his co-authors discussed were quickly infiltrating the entire order. Aware of this potentially devastating influence, we entitled a special section of the document "From Individualism to the Prophetic Witness of Fraternity." The document states:

> The causes of individualism cannot be isolated in a way that points fingers to this or that reason or at this or that person. Our individualism mirrors society, whether in the East or West, the North or the South. Despite slogans about freedom and equality, and commitment to solidarity, forces subtly develop forms of collectivization through political control of the media and economic dominance through advertising. Both forms result in increased glorification of individualism....
>
> All this has had its effect on our fraternities as well.... The consequence is an erosion of bonds of fraternity among us, a tendency to give priority to community elsewhere and, again, increasing individualism.[43]

The marginalized survivors of our political economy as well as the innocent victims of our clericalized church certainly are aching to hear authentic prophetic voices that might bring them some good news. But the voices of religious will never be heard, much less acted upon, if we remain part and parcel of the dominant consciousness of individualism that presently sustains the ever-more-globalized milieu in which we live. To develop any "prophetic voice" and to have this nurtured in "prophetic communities," we need to examine more deeply the nature of prophecy and its antithesis in the dominant culture.

To define oneself a prophet or one's group as prophetic without protesting the dominant culture's or church's undermining the power of God's word does a disservice to the Scriptures, violates our founders' vision, and bankrupts us before God's people. To allow this split between theory and practice, between one's cultural mores and one's personal morality to continue dishonors the immanence of the Creating One at the heart of creation. However, to stand as loving critics of the sinful structures around us because we are energized in the spirit to form alternative communities of conscience is to embrace Jesus' call to conversion in a radically alternative way.

Another phenomenon that affects our ability as "mainline" religious to function collectively as prophetic revolves around our aging. At the 2004 Assembly of the LCWR and CMSM, statistics were presented indicating that there are more women religious over the age of ninety than there are under fifty.

If we are to become "prophetic," I believe we can be helped by a deeper examination of the prophetic persons and messages of Isaiah (1–39), Jeremiah, and Ezekiel. In their witness we can find the core ingredients of what it means to live ethical lives in a corrupting political economy; from them we can see to be open to the Spirit in a religious institution that proclaims itself the paragon of morality but too often witnesses to arrogance and abuse of power. In the study of their call, their message, and their witness we will find the constitutive elements of what it means to live a moral life in an immoral society.

Edith Wyschogrod writes: "To lead a moral life one does not need a theory about how one should live, but a flesh and blood existent."[44] I believe First Isaiah, Jeremiah, and Ezekiel are three human beings, three holy people, who put flesh and blood on what it means to be moral, what it means to be holy, what it means to be faithful to God in an unfaithful generation. To their witness we will now turn in our next three chapters.

Two

The Mystical/Prophetic Vocation
of Isaiah

Isaiah's Call as Prototype

Isaiah's vocation occurred in 742 BCE, the year King Uzziah of Judah died. Using powerful, almost apocalyptic images, the prophet describes what happened to him when his mystical, prophetic call came to him:

> In the year that King Uzziah died, I saw the Lord sitting on a throne, high and lofty; and the hem of his robe filled the temple. Seraphs were in attendance above him; each had six wings: with two they covered their faces, and with two they covered their feet, and with two they flew. And one called to another and said:
>
> > Holy, holy, holy is the Lord of hosts;
> > the whole earth is full of his glory.
>
> The pivots on the thresholds shook at the voices of those who called, and the house filled with smoke. And I said: "Woe is me! I am lost, for I am a man of unclean lips, and I live among a people of unclean lips; yet my eyes have seen the King, the Lord of hosts!"
> Then one of the seraphs flew to me, holding a live coal that had been taken from the altar with a pair of tongs. The seraph touched my mouth with it and said: "Now that this has touched your lips, your guilt has departed and your sin is blotted out." Then I heard the voice of the Lord saying, "Whom shall I send, and who will go for us?" (Isa. 6:1–8a).

Up to now, according to Isaiah, everything about his mystical call appeared to be wonderful and awesome. Even at the point where he "heard

the voice of the Lord saying, 'Whom shall I send; who will go for us?'"
the observer might feel inspired to begin singing the words of the contemporary hymn: "Here I am Lord, I have heard you calling in the night.
I will go Lord, if you lead me."[1]

Would that the prophetic call was this charming!

Isaiah's vision presented him with an entirely new consciousness of
God's holiness and evoked in him a deep sense of his own unholiness,
of how far short he fell from divine glory. It also made him immediately
conscious, seemingly for the first time, of the sinfulness around him, of
what in his society profaned the holiness of God. Overwhelmed by this
holiness, he came to a new understanding of what was truly "unclean," and
so, being made critically conscious of authentic holiness, he found himself
grounded in and operating from a new moral sensitivity. Aware that his
co-religionists would insist on their traditional understanding of what it
means to be holy, he assured himself that he had truly been touched by
God's true holiness. Empowered by God's word, he felt compelled to go
to his own people and call them to take up a life of true holiness.

However, sustained as they are by a culture that blinds them from seeing
its injustice, deafens them to the cry of the poor, and ritually sanctions
sin and abuse in the name of religion, Isaiah finds them ideologically
convinced of their righteousness. Given their cultural captivity, the voice
tells him that his preaching would fall on closed eyes and deaf ears. His
people's hearts are "hardened," a biblical image that we might today call
sociological apathy or anomie.

When Isaiah asked "How long, O Lord," God answered that his prophetic vocation would not be concluded until cities would lie in waste
without inhabitants and the land would be "utterly desolate" with everyone being sent "far away." Only one ray of hope would be allowed to
break through: the only thing left standing would be the stump of an oak,
which would be a holy seed (Isa. 6:11–13) from which new life would
come forth out of the death of the old. A remnant would remain, and
a refounding community would take the place of the unrepentant priests
and their institution.

Isaiah's call instructs us that God's holiness is the only criterion for a
moral life in individuals or in institutions. Old Testament scholar Peter
Ellis suggests that all of Isaiah's "major ideas can best be appreciated"

from the perspective of "this vision of God's holiness" in chapter 6, verses 1–13. Everything before anticipates this vision, and all that comes after is its result. Isaiah's experience of God's holiness empowered him with a new understanding of God's nature, and this new vision enabled him to speak to his world from that experience in a way that exposed that world's structural alienation from this holiness. So much did his experience and understanding of God as "holy" affect his person and his proclamation that, for Ellis, Isaiah stands in history as "the prophet of holiness."[2]

Given this stress on Isaiah's prophetic vocation as grounded in the mystical experience of God's holiness, I would like to examine in greater detail the implications of this foundational text, pursue a "deep reading" of Isaiah 6, and draw out more fully the implications this text has for our own mystical/prophetic call to live in our nation and religion, our territory and temple, in a way that no longer immunizes us from what God truly requires of us.

The fact that Isaiah was born during the prosperous but immoral reign of King Uzziah (784–742) gives his vision more relevance for us who live in the most prosperous nations on the face of this earth, including those of us in the "American Empire" itself. If we would be honest and not blinded by ideology, we must admit that much of our prosperity has been achieved and is being maintained at the expense of the poor and the planet. That such oppression and exploitation do not deeply concern us is evidence of our own hard-heartedness, to use the prophet's phrase, our cultural alienation from the God whose presence breathes at the heart of all creation, even if we give continual lip service to God and tell ourselves that we are the most divinely blessed of all the nations. Thus the nature of Isaiah's vision has profound relevance for us religious who are called to live as mystics and prophets in the midst of our political economy with its imperial pomposity and our institutional church with its posture of infallibility.

Evelyn Underhill notes that the elements contained in Isaiah's experience of God's holiness constitute the heart of every prophetic/mystical vocation.[3] These core elements are the same two that constitute religious life, according to the 1989 meeting of U.S. leaders of women's and men's religious congregations: the prophetic stance that arises from and is nurtured by a contemplative attitude.

Certainly such a connection between mystical contemplation and prophetic action is true for us religious who are Franciscans. Francis's own experience of the seraphs granting him the stigmata at Mt. Alverna has always been interpreted as the culmination of his call to enflesh the Gospel of Jesus Christ in his thirteenth-century world where empire and *ekklēsía* vied for hegemony over the universe. The details of this episode in his life are redolent in many ways of Isaiah's own mystical encounter.

In 1226, two years before his death, Francis made a retreat at Mt. Alverna. As he reflected on Jesus' passion and death, he experienced a deep desire to be joined with Christ in his suffering. According to the *Little Flowers,* Francis found himself praying:

> My Lord Jesus Christ, I pray You to grant me two graces before I die: the first is that during my life I may feel in my soul and in my body, as much as possible, that pain which You, dear Jesus, sustained in the hour of Your most bitter passion. The second is that I may feel in my heart, as much as possible, that excessive love with which You, O Son of God, were inflamed in willingly enduring such suffering for us sinners.[4]

As he saw the seraph flying toward him in the form of one crucified, Francis experienced two emotions: great fear on the one hand and overwhelming joy on the other. Within these contrasting emotions, he experienced coming from the seraph rays that enfleshed in him the mark of the Crucified One. What he had espoused, he now experienced. What he experienced, Francis now embodied in his person.

As we consider Francis's vision at Mt. Alverna in the light of the story of Isaiah's mystical/prophetic call and how these powerful experiences might be nurtured in our lives, I find seven elements that constitute biblical holiness in the life of one called to be a prophet:

The Call Occurs within Concrete Historical Exigencies: "In the Year That King Uzziah Died" (Isa. 6:1a)

Unlike those who want religion to be divorced from reality or who favor a church removed from culture or one that accepts the surrounding culture without critique, Isaiah's vision makes it clear that all authentic spirituality must be lived *in the world as it is.* Our call to be prophetic takes place within the present reality, which in turn demands that we understand the present "signs of the times" as quite different from those of the "glory days" of religious life in the West. In my mind, few if any religious writing today on our call as religious have articulated the crisis we currently face as we try to embrace the world we have come to know from physics, astronomy, and cosmology. One exception is Barbara Fiand, who contends that, as we move into an awareness of the holistic and complementary connectedness of our universe, our spirituality has not kept apace. She writes: "Dualistic spirituality, which is dominant in our church even to this day, holds within it both the hierarchical as well as the patriarchal view of the sacred." The consequences are isolating us from relevance in the real world, she argues:

> We face today the results of a dualistic, patriarchal, and hierarchi-cal spirituality. It permeates still, even after Vatican II, our liturgies and prayers, our ecclesial structures and mandates, our church's of-ficial presence in the world, and many of the structures of religious life. We were all reared in it, trained as religious to see through its set of glasses, judge with its measuring sticks, weigh with its scales. So used to it are we that many of us might balk in disbelief and consternation at the suggestion that there can be another way of interpreting reality, another way of experiencing ourselves and our relation to each other, the world, and God — a way equally valid and profoundly Chrisitan, but holistic rather than dualistic, incarnational rather than disembodied.[5]

This dominant culture and its accompanying ideology are sustained by what Brueggemann calls the "royal consciousness." Hegemonic in nature, it allows no alternative views. Politically, the dominant culture is sus-tained by the idolatry of U.S. imperial power buttressed by military might. It stresses self-reliance at the expense of others. It is ensured economically by the idolatry of Adam Smith's invisible hand. Its sanctification of self-reliance can be realized only at the expense of the poor and marginalized. Religiously, this ideology is canonized by a church that issues statements *about* the "world's" injustices and immorality but too often will not support its members who challenge these injustices, because their methods might unsettle benefactors. Under the guise of infallible truth, a clericalized church makes common cause with patriarchal interests in a way opposite to prophetic transformation.

As Israel itself was seduced by the patterns of the people it sought to conquer, we find that in the year of our Uzziahs — be they presidents or popes — we have become the bearers and beneficiaries of an increasingly globalized body; in fact as "Americans" our social location places us at the heart of this globalization. For this reason, the experience of any prophetic call must be expressed within an ever-expanding and interconnected universe in which the politics of oppression belies fundamental justice, economic dynamics enable the rich to be richer at the expense of the poor, and an ecclesiastical system promotes a vision of God that denies God's inclusive and equalizing trinitarian love for all.

When I consider more deeply the reality of the universe within which our contemporary Uzziahs operate, I find four levels constituting what we can call our "world." None of them can be absent from the power of God's reign. First is what I call the "individual" level of our world, the level of our own personal lives. Then there are our relationships, the "interpersonal" level of life, our communities, our families, our work places, and our neighborhoods. We find then the level of systems and structures, the "infrastructural" level, which represents how our institutions organize and ensure a certain distribution of power and resources. These patterns are promoted and protected via the dominant ideology. Finally, at the deepest level we find the universe itself; this is the "environmental" level.

Isaiah tells us his call took place in the year King Uzziah died, and it came to him while he was in a house. The fact that his vocation came to him in a "house" is significant. The Greek word for house is *oikía* or *oikos*. In the Mediterranean world that provided the context for his writing, "house," or *oikía,* did not mean so much a building as a whole "world," or network of interconnected relationships at every level of life. These relationships defined the ordering of all sorts of resources among various persons. There being no word for "family" in Greek, *oikía* and *oikos* represented the core unit of society. As such its dynamics would make or break the entire system.

A household's various expressions became manifest according to the different ways of ordering relationships among persons and their resources at every level. The Greek word for "order" is *nomos*. Consequently house-ordering (*oikos* + *nomos*) constituted that world's economy (*oikonomía*). In that "world," economics, at the second level, involved the ordering of resources among various persons. Later, in the milieu that gave rise to the community identified with Jesus of Nazareth, the same persons who related to each other with their resources (*oikonomía*) in a way that reflected his vision of God's household came to be called *ekklēsía*. *Oikía* also is the root word for the third level of the world, the infrastructure. This is the *oikoumēne*, or inhabited part of our ecumenical or interactive life. Finally the relational dynamics of *oikía* encompasses the fourth level of our world, the *oikología* or the environment itself.

Only by living in right relationships with all of this "world" at its four levels will we be able to experience with Isaiah the inbreaking of God's trinitarian presence at the heart of the universe.[6] It will only be when we become brothers and sisters to "all in the house" (*oikía, okonomía,* and *oikoumēne*) that we will live with credibility at the heart of the *oikología*. It will only be when we realize that the integrity of the *oikología* in and around us demands prophetic challenges to whatever in the *oikoumēne* undermines the universal integrity of the *oikología* itself that we will be promoting the kind of *oikonomía* that reflects the trinitarian reign of our God.

When I entered religious life in 1959 I was told that I was "leaving the world." Every effort was made to separate me from its network of relations. Now I know from quantum theory, chaos theory, and my own understanding of God as an economic trinity-at-the-heart-of-all-reality that this world exists within my own being, my own *oikía*. As I write this book more than forty years after "leaving the world," I have discovered that the only way I can be a religious is to define my life in relation to the world in and around me and to be prepared to enter into its core with the mystical/prophetic vision of Isaiah embedded in my depths. I can never be removed from "the world," for it is at the core of my being. Religious life at one time may have been able to survive apart from "the world"; now religious know, with all true seekers, that the spiritual life can be worthy of the term "spiritual" only when it exists as an energizing force, the very spirit that enables the heart of world to vibrate with life. Even the vows, as Alexandra Kovats has shown so powerfully, must be revisioned from this holistic (i.e., totally holy) perspective.[7]

At the Second Synod of Bishops, in 1971, the delegates discussed the "signs of the times" and "listened to the Word of God" in a way that led them to offer a disturbing analysis of "the situation of the world." Coming to Rome from all parts of the globe, they said their common reflections led them "to perceive the serious injustices which are building around the world of men a network of domination, oppression and abuses which stifle freedom and which keep the greater part of humanity from sharing in the building up and enjoyment of a more just and more fraternal world."[8] Given this ever-increasing globalization of dynamics that dehumanize people and foster inequity, they went on to say that action "on behalf of justice" now had to be considered constitutive for any who proclaimed to be living and witnessing to the Gospel.[9]

At the heart of the prophetic vocation is the call for right relationships throughout the universe, justice in a political economy that increasing numbers around the world view as constitutively unjust,[10] and greater solidarity in a church whose leaders' own abuses have done as much spiritual violence to many believers as has the corporate violence done to the citizenry. Thus the bishops' own words about the need for justice in the world, including the church, demand that some in the church respond to this call in a special, corporate, way. Who is more suited than those who proclaim their vocation to constitute the mystical/prophetic vocation itself?

This Call Imprints on Our Consciousness the Reality of God's Own Holiness (Isa. 6:1b–4)

Isaiah writes that he "saw the Lord sitting on a throne, high and lofty" (Isa. 6:1b). Such language reinforces for many the primitive anthropology of God as located in some geographic place called "heaven" that exists beyond the dome of the heavens that covered the earth. However, the prophet's choice of words merely expresses in human language the ineffable, indescribable experience Isaiah had of being transported into the vision of God's ultimate transcendence. His "seeing" was his experience of God's holiness.

As we entered the third millennium, with its relevations of sexual abuse by priests and power abuse by bishops, we heard a lot of talk and read even more words about the need for "holiness." If the voices from Rome and the U.S.-based neoconservatives would be believed, the lack of holiness in our church by the clergy seems to have created the crisis. While I agree on the need for "holiness," what these voices mean by "sanctity" does not adequately reflect Isaiah's experience of it. Their notion of holiness or sanctity is overly conflated with fidelity, which in turn is virtually synonymous with "orthodox" allegiance to what I call "the Church of Matthew 16." It seems to be a contemporary mirror of the holiness codes that ensured group separation that Jesus declared to be outside the reign or way of God (Matt. 5:20–48). Unless our "holiness" exceeds that of our contemporary scribes and Pharisees, it's not likely any of us will be reflecting the dynamics of what Jesus called the "kingdom of God." Holiness in Matthew's Gospel is another word for justice. This justice demands a spirituality that goes beyond the holiness codes of any generation if they undermine God's trinitarian life at the heart of all reality.

Once we experience the reign, the realm, the reality, and indeed the rush of God's presence and power breaking into our lives, all else becomes relativized, an illusion. Once we get a glimpse of God's trinitarian reality and how this God has chosen to be with us in all our relationships, our lives can only be spent longing to make this God the core of our being and the center of our world. Once we experience God's trinitarian holiness, our former ideas of sanctity, of one group's superiority over another, one class above another, one body ontologically superior to the other, one higher than another, is seen for what it is: an unholy and even sinful ideology at odds with God's unity. With the universal call to holiness no one nor any group can be considered "more holy" or consecrated in a way that sets them apart from and, especially, "above" any others if that means "lording it over them."

The experience of God that we express in our world on all its levels through our participation in community is what I call spirituality. Spirituality represents the way we reflect the holiness of God; it is our way of being holy in the contemporary world. However, while such spirituality demands that we *express* this holiness in an unholy world, its foundation is in our *experience* of the holy that makes us look at the world in a new way. This experience of the holy is another name for contemplation. Without contemplation, the experience of the holy, there can be little or no authentic prophetic utterance.

"Holy, holy, holy is the Lord of hosts; the whole earth is full of his glory," Isaiah heard one of the seraphs call to another (6:3). "Holiness" derives from the Old English word *hâlignes,* meaning to be without blemish or injury. It parallels the Hebrew word *qds* and the Greek *hagios,* which involve being consecrated in a way that sets one apart from that which is considered sinful or profane (see also the Hebrew *kabod* and the Greek *doxa*). The Hebrew Scriptures outline three related ways one could be holy. The *wisdom* writers highlighted the need for individual integrity in the sight of God, the *prophets* stressed the need to make a connection between worship, social justice, and conversion, and the *priestly school* insisted on observable separation for cult along with the practice of the "holiness code" in order to fulfill the scriptural imperative: "You shall be holy, for I the Lord your God am holy" (Lev. 19:2).

Holiness pertains to the witness of a moral life lived justly in the midst of immorality. This justice was to characterize all relationships involving the morality of individuals, households, and the people themselves. Personal holiness was inseparable from right relationships at all levels of the household among people and the earth's resources. God's holiness was to be translated into human behavior in a way that set people apart from others whether these others were individuals or systems — even if this meant excluding oneself or one's group from the dynamics of the reigning political economy and religion. As Norbert Lohfink writes, the call for Israel to be holy (moral) in the way God is, meant the practice of an "alternative social character over against the societies of the world. As the Holy One, God is 'Wholly Other.' Thus, the Israel that submitted to his lordship [over all creation] should also be 'wholly other' from the peoples. Since this otherness should reach into all dimensions [of the world], an alternative form of economy is itself implied."[11]

By the time of Jesus, the Holiness Codes no longer served as a critique of the unholy systems in which the Jewish people found themselves. Rather these laws had become encapsulated in highly detailed rules and regulations whose moral imperatives were quite individualistic. They ensured the separation of the classes of people by divine fiat. The detailed observance of these codes by religion's adherents determined whether a person would be defined as holy or unholy, clean or unclean, pure or impure, in or out. Consequently, with his alternative approach to Torah and table Jesus redefined "holiness" as a way of compassionate relationship to others at all levels of life.[12] While I will develop this notion of compassion more fully later, here I want to highlight what we have come to know about God's *way of being holy* or interrelated. We call this the Trinity.

The core of our Christian faith revolves around the notion of God's holiness within God's self (the immanent trinity) and as it has been revealed to us (the economic trinity). This we call the *Holy* Trinity. In the "Blessed" Trinity each person is God precisely because each relates to the other in a way that enables each to have total access to the other's resources. From our experience gained from the Scriptures and tradition, this is called the "*economic* Trinity." These three *persons* are in *relationship* to each other in such a way that every *resource* available to the one is totally for the other; there is no appropriation of any resource by any one person at the expense of any other person. In this mutuality and solidarity rests the fulness of the Godhead. This pattern not only defines the way the Holy Trinity exists and functions; it constitutes the Blessed Economy (or "house ordering") that is the trinitarian God.

Isaiah's experience of God was of the One beyond all imagination; our understanding of God's oneness today is that of a triune community. Once we have our Isaiah experience of God's holiness manifest in this way, it necessarily constitutes the leitmotif for how we view all reality and relationships — whether they be personal or interpersonal, economic or political, cultural or religious. Even from a faith-based approach to quantum physics and the new science, the trinitarian godhead exists as the energy that underlies all other relationships, the power that lies at the heart of everything that is, the archetype of creation itself.

Awareness that all reality is interrelated and grounded in God not only constitutes the heart of the contemplative experience; it characterizes what the LCWR and CMSM termed to be the "contemplative attitude toward life." This means, they said, that religious must be "attentive to and motivated by the presence of the sacred in their own inner journeys, in the lives of others, and throughout creation." The ability to critique all reality in light of the sacred, the holiness of God, the Blessed Trinity, is the lens that provides the vision for all religious. It is how they are called to *see*. The desire to witness to that Trinity in the way they relate to each other as persons with their resources shared in common will be the sign of the authenticity of their religious experience.

Our current economics, politics, and ecclesiastical ordering of relations among persons and resources fails to measure up to the *imago dei* that must be trinitarian — universally communal and interrelated. To the degree they fail in their way of ordering relationships and resources among persons, people of faith must consider them opposed to the holiness of God's name, the reign of God as well as the will of God. The fact that the culture's and the church's dominant consciousness often justifies what can be less-than-godliness demands that, when this takes place, those rationales and programs that deny trinitarian relationships must be unmasked as sinful and their ideological rationalization be exposed as a lie.

The experience of God's holiness demands in a special way that religious — who with the whole church are called to be holy — announce that all holiness must reflect that holiness of God that empowers and energizes everything in creation. At the same time they must denounce whatever stands opposed to the image of the trinitarian God whom they experience and know to be at the heart of all that is; anything short of this at any level of creation must be invited to conversion. As Pope John Paul II wrote about religious as prophetic:

> True prophecy is born of God, from friendship with him, from attentive listening to his word in the different circumstances of history. Prophets feel in their hearts a burning desire for the holiness of God and, having heard his word in the dialogue of prayer, they proclaim that word in their lives, with their lips and with their actions, becoming people who speak for God against evil and sin. Prophetic witness requires the constant and passionate search for God's will, for self-giving, for unfailing communion in the Church, for the practice of spiritual discernment and love of the truth. It is also expressed through the denunciation of all that is contrary to the divine will and through the exploration of new ways to apply the Gospel in history, in expectation of the coming of God's Kingdom.[13]

The words of Pope John Paul II about prophets being grounded in the experience of God make it clear that from this experience the prophet discovers a new criterion for God's will-in-the-world. Anything in human relationships that fails to measure up to this vision must be recognized as violating God's holiness; to that degree it is sinful. This brings me to the next element that created Isaiah's prophetic consciousness and subsequent voice.

Experiencing God's Holiness Gives Us an Enlightened Consciousness of Sin in Its Individual and Social Manifestations (Isa. 6:5)

> Woe is me! I am lost, for I am a man of unclean lips, and I live among a people of unclean lips; yet my eyes have seen the King, the Lord of hosts!

In response to his experience of true holiness, Isaiah the priest came to realize how far from God he and his people had moved. Consequently, he could only respond: "Woe is me! I am lost, for I am a man of unclean lips." At the same time, his own awareness of how he was falling short of God's glory made him deeply conscious of sin all around him. Thus, he added: "and I live among a people of unclean lips." His new moral consciousness distanced him from the dominant religious understanding of "holiness" prevalent at that time. Given his co-religionists' conviction that their way was God's way and, therefore, moral and holy, Isaiah realized they would never grasp what he now knew: what they called "grace" was not only deeply flawed, but seriously sinful. Only one who experienced what was truly holy would be able to understand: "yet my eyes have seen the King, the Lord of hosts!" His mystical experience forced him to "see" in a way that marginalized him from his social institutions and their ideologies. As Sandra Schneiders, I.H.M., writes of today's prophets: "Contemplative immediacy to God and social marginality are the coordinates of religious life as a prophetic life form in the Church" today.[14]

From his vision of the heavens Isaiah's recognition of sin in and around him led him immediately to a new vision for living on earth. In looking at his own life and that of the world around him, his conscience had been stirred to understand holiness from a new perspective, through a new moral lens, a new perspective of whether he and his world were living rightly and justly.

Until this experience of God's holiness, Isaiah seems to have taken for granted the world of meaning that had been mediated to him through the dominant consciousness of his culture, in which a particular political economy was sanctioned by the religious leadership of his day. With his experience of *God's* holiness, all that changed. His mystical vision generated in him a gut-wrenching stirring of conscience that resulted in a new moral imperative.

Today, as in Isaiah's time, false consciousness also leads to faulty conscience. Our own economic system is blessed as the allocation of scarce resources among competing persons to meet unlimited wants. But few of us seem to question how the desires of some few people in power can be guaranteed in ways that deny the basic needs of countless others and undermine the integrity of creation itself. Only when we hear stories about one corporate executive after another making sure his interests are served, even as whole corporations founder, do we begin to wonder what's wrong. And even then, to keep us from critiquing a system that closed its heart to the sin, we are assured that such behavior represents only a few bad apples or that the media has exploited the situation.

Or, in another manifestation of false consciousness creating faulty conscience, we find the Roman Catholic church leaders, supposedly teachers of the truth, say it is God's will that women be denied full access to all the sacraments. Unable to argue that there is any clear mandate from God for this position in the Scriptures, they conclude instead that they have not received any power from God to change the historical pattern in which women may be images of God, but not in *persona Christi,* the *divine* one.

Or yet another example. When the bishops of the Catholic Church met in synod in 1971 to examine how people were being oppressed and how resources were being allocated in ways that ensured that the rich were getting richer and the poor were getting poorer across the world, they stated that this phenomenon, in their eyes, represented a "grave sin of injustice."[15] Upon further introspection, they even conceded that this injustice may possibly be supported by the structure of the church itself. Aware of this dichotomy between what is taught and what is frequently done, they stated: "While the Church is bound to give witness to justice, she recognizes that anyone who ventures to speak to people about justice must first be just in their eyes. Hence we must undertake an examination of the modes of acting and of the possessions and life style found within the Church itself."[16] Elements in any such "examination," they went on to say, involved respect for basic human rights including women's share and participation in the church and a guarantee of fair judicial procedures.

Because unfettered corporate capitalism insists its ways are the only ways to ensure free markets, and because imperial politics believes the "American Way" is sanctioned by God, it's hard to penetrate people's consciousness with another vision of what might be right or just; its adherents have become numbed to any alternative vision. While this is so with our political economy, it seems even more the case when we consider the clerical consciousness that controls the Roman Catholic Church. That it might be possible for our leaders to be wrong is unthinkable to many; after all, didn't Jesus promise to be with the church "always, to the end of the age" (Matt. 28:20)? We forget, however, what Isaiah reminds us: a similar promise was made to Israel, and yet it lost its territory and temple and was taken into exile.

In the prophet's time and ours, the dominance of a cultural and clerical consciousness undermines the possibility of thinking differently. Given the dominance of such imperial and infallible thinking, Isaiah himself could well have doubted himself if he had begun to think in a way contrary to the ideology around him. But the truth of his vision and the moral imperative for all creation which that entailed became for him a new consciousness and a new conscience. Everything that failed to measure up to this divine vision would now be called by him what it in fact was: idolatry. What before had been considered grace would now be denounced as, in fact, a disgrace to God! What once had been considered holy would now be rejected as a profanation of the divine presence.

As Isaiah said, "My eyes have seen the King, the Lord of hosts" (Isa. 6:5b). In other words the truth of what he experienced revealed the lie that had been sustaining the political, economic, and religious world which once had given him meaning. Never again could he look at these forces with the same eyes, hear their message with the same ears, or accept their ways with the same heart. Why? Simply because he had understood with his heart and experienced a radical conversion.

Too often conversion has been thought of as a "turning away." Isaiah's conversion was different, a resounding "yes" rather than a simple "no." In a full and complete surrender to his experience of God's holiness, Isaiah came to embrace a divine stance toward the world, such that whatever stood apart from this became profane and all that reflected this holiness had to be affirmed and supported.

The Recognition of Sin in Our Lives Opens Us to Be Healed and Empowered by a Force beyond Us: The Word of God (Isa. 6:6–7)

If we cannot acknowledge we are sinners, we will never be converted, and in refusing to see the need for conversion, we remain the same. If we stay the same, we will remain in our sins. Righteous in our sins, we can easily convince ourselves that we are holy. Unable to see how far short we are of measuring up to God's holiness, we will never be empowered to live holy lives if what profanes our lives controls our thinking about them. I know the seduction of this "royal" and "papal" consciousness from my own experience.

I was at a juncture in my life where I was not consciously sinning (or, with Martin Luther, if I did sin, I sinned "boldly" and "confessed boldly"). Not aware of any sin on my part, I developed unconsciously a kind of righteous certainty that I was living in the reign of God, and this righteousness of mine made me quite proud of myself. At this point I was challenged by prophetic words coming from a Franciscan sister by the name of Janet Sullivan. One day I heard her say, "We've moved far from the spiritual path when we no longer think we need salvation." Hello! This was me.

I had told myself I was not sinning; therefore I was graced. Not sinning, I didn't need to change. No longer sinning, I no longer needed a savior. I no longer needed God; I had made myself God. Such a realization brought fresh insight into Jesus' words in Matthew to those righteous religious leaders who could not imagine they were doing anything wrong but, instead, could only point fingers at him for his aberrations that put him outside their law: "Those who are well have no need of a physician, but those who are sick. Go and learn what this means, 'I desire mercy, not sacrifice.' For I have come to call not the righteous but sinners" (Matt. 9:12–13).

My experience gave me a fresh understanding of how Isaiah, only after he recognized his own sin and could admit it publicly, could be open to be healed of its influence and hold over his life. Only then could he say, "One of the seraphs flew to me, holding a live coal that had been taken from the altar with a pair of tongs. The seraph touched my mouth with it and said: 'Now that this has touched your lips, your guilt has departed and your sin is blotted out'" (Isa. 6:6). Not only did the coal — which most take to represent God's word — heal Isaiah of his own sinfulness; it empowered him to live from its force. This empowerment, in fact, enabled his original experience of the vision of God's holiness to become embodied in his very being. He who had experienced true holiness was now freed from his own unholiness by acknowledging it. Now, in the power of this word grounding him in God's holiness, he could be commissioned to proclaim an authentic holiness to a sinful nation.

Too often conversion has been thought of as a "turning away." Isaiah's conversion was different, a resounding "yes" rather than a simple "no."

In the next chapter I will discuss a parallel incident in Jeremiah's life when, despite his reluctance and even resistance, he allowed himself to be overtaken by God's powerful word in his life (Jer. 1:4ff). Suffice it to be said here that, once we truly experience the blessedness or holiness of God's life, this supraordinate reality cannot be anything but the leitmotif by which we judge everything else. Anything falling short of this Word, this revelation, this holiness is, to that degree, unholy or profane. The experience of God's healing word in us invites us to live reordered lives. It also serves as a mandate to spend our lives challenging whatever in our world — be it the culture itself or our religious system — stands outside our understanding of God's word (Isa. 6:7).

One would think that the notion of God's holiness being the criterion by which everything around us would be judged would be especially true within our religious institutions. Sadly and too often, the leaders of our religious institutions, especially those in my own Roman Catholic faith, can be the most resistant. Somehow, one would think, the institutional church, as the very institution that should be the model of right-ordering or justice ought to be the most likely place one who has experienced God's holiness should be able to speak one's truth. One would think that any persecution for speaking one's truth would come more from the forces that define the political economy than those who are leaders in the church. But as Jesus himself acknowledged, prophets are usually without honor among their own. As a result they feel even more estranged from their society and religious institutions. Sandra Schneiders writes:

> Part of the agony of the prophet arises from a visceral sense that whatever persecution one might have to suffer *should* come from ungodly, worldly, or sinful structures or people. Persecution by the church always feels wrong. There is a nagging suspicion that if one were truly advancing God's agenda the church, at least, would be approving and supporting one's efforts. Rejection and oppression by the ecclesiastical institution is the most subversive force in the life of the Religious, the most undermining experience of the Religious congregation.[17]

Given the institutional constraints noted in the previous chapter, whether or not we religious can become this needed prophetic voice is debatable. However, I have become convinced that only a prophetic voice will give us true moral credibility as it did with Isaiah and later Jesus himself. At issue is whether we are willing to move from a way of being religious that reinforces the dominant consciousness to another, more prophetic mode of religious life, to being loving critics of society and church. As Joan Chittister writes: "What is yet to be seen in our generation is whether or not the religious of this age are free enough of their present cultural heritage of privatism, individual development, individualism and personal religion to pursue a new set of values themselves." This new way of being religious demands leaving the territory and temple of power and privilege that has sustained us. It means that we would begin to challenge the "sin of our world." She states:

> Past value systems of achievement, security, and national parochial-ism have resulted in peaks of economic domination, militarism, and national chauvinism that is bringing the West to a new kind of moral degeneration. What is needed now is a model of political compas-sion, universalism, an ecology of life, justice and peace if the planet

is to survive and all its people are to live decent human lives. What is yet to be discovered is whether the religious of this time either hold these values themselves or will dedicate themselves to making them evident for others.[18]

Until now few religious, much less religious communities, have embraced their mystical/prophetic call in any sustained and wholistic way. In light of Chittister's words, such an absence of prophetic action would lead one to question whether the religious of this time who claim to be contemplatives have even experienced the God of Isaiah. Are we still locked into serving a god who is patriarchal and hierarchical rather than relational and communal? Can we "see" the Holy Trinity?

Empowered in This Word, We Accept the Invitation to Go into the World as God's Ambassadors (Isa. 6:8)

Isaiah's experience of the burning coal made him realize that he was not just freed of his past sins; God's word had been implanted in him so that he might proclaim it to the world. At the heart of every mystical/prophetic call is the demand that one's experience of God be brought forward to the world in an entirely new way. The true prophet proclaims the sovereignty of God's presence and power in the midst of contrary imperial pretensions and infallible proclamations. Thus Pope John Paul II in *Vita Consecrata* writes:

> In our world, where it often seems that the signs of God's presence have been lost from sight, a convincing prophetic witness on the part of consecrated persons is increasingly necessary. In the first place this should entail the affirmation of the primacy of God and of eternal life.... Consecrated persons are being asked to bear witness everywhere with the boldness of a prophet who is unafraid of risking even his life.[19]

In Old Testament times, establishment prophecy revolved around inductive and intuitive divination derived from a nonhuman source.[20] One method was the prophet's inference of divine intention, as gleaned from various events (e.g., tears in the eyes of an ox, pigs gnashing their teeth).

The problem with this kind of divination was that it could be easily manipulated to get the desired yes or no from "God." Another form of prophecy
occurred when the prophets spoke a message received in some dream or
insight as though they themselves were the source of the message. The
problem with this form of divination is that one would not know until the
event took place whether the prophecy was true or false.

While such lesser forms of "prophecy" can easily suffer from human
whim, truly divine inspiration is different. True prophecy proclaims God's
project for people and the planet, especially in a world that has deviated
from God. The prophet's words present God's larger agenda for justice
in a world that has strayed from the Word. Thus, true prophecy speaks
on behalf of God, which makes this prophecy very different from simple
divination or even ordinary religious experience. Heschel writes:

> Religious experience, in most cases, is a private affair in which a per-
> son becomes alive to what transpires between God and himself, not
> to what transpires between God and someone else; contact between
> God and man comes about, it is believed, for the benefit of the par-
> ticular man. In contrast, prophetic inspiration is for the sake, for the
> benefit, of a third party. It is not a private affair between prophet
> and God; its purpose is the illumination of the people rather than
> the illumination of the prophet.[21]

"Whom shall I send, who will go for us," God asks? This is a question
all people called to the prophetic vocation must not only be open to
hear; reluctant as they may be, they also must be willing to act upon the
invitation.

Being commissioned by God is the source of a prophet's consecration. One is sent to others on behalf of the sender. The message is a
call to transformation; the messenger is merely the conduit, the one who
calls for conversion — but on God's terms, not one's own. In effect, the
prophet is the ambassador of God, the one whose words are divinely authorized. Divinely inspired prophets speak with power because they have
been empowered to proclaim it, be that proclamation one of words or
works, gesture or symbol.

Given a Christian understanding of the Incarnation as God coming
among us in human form, Jesus of Nazareth is God's most complete ambassador, and in turn through their baptismal call, Christ's disciples are

sent to be his ambassadors, his witnesses in the world as well. Empowered by his Spirit, we are to continue the teaching of Christ, proclaiming his good news of God's reign in our empires and the healing of sickness and disease of every kind — no matter where they may be found in individuals, groups, and institutions (Matt. 4:23; 9:35). In other words, we are to incarnate the living message of God in ways that will bring good news to the poor as well as serve notice to the petty gods of empire and *ekklēsía* that they no longer can claim our dutiful worship and unquestioning obeisance. Whether or not they receive us well is not the point: being commissioned, we must feel compelled to speak of what we have experienced. We are sent as ambassadors of Christ: "Whoever welcomes you welcomes me, and whoever welcomes me welcomes the one who sent me. Whoever welcomes a prophet in the name of a prophet will receive a prophet's reward; and whoever welcomes a righteous person in the name of a righteous person will receive the reward of the righteous" (10:40–41).

In examining the charisms granted to the founders of most religious congregations, we often find precisely this sense of being called as witnesses of God, God's ambassadors to the world. For instance, Francis's "Testament" documents the special insight into God that Francis received when he embraced the leper, his own version, so to speak, of what Isaiah described in chapter 6. By allowing himself to be led by God and renouncing allegiance to his society's ideology, especially its rejection of the sick and unclean, Francis lived from an entirely new vision, a prophetic vision. It influenced the rest of his life. In his own words, he said of this experience: "This is how God inspired me, Brother Francis, to embark upon a life of penance. When I was in sin, the sight of lepers nauseated me beyond measure; but then God himself led me into their company, and I had pity on them. When I had once become acquainted with them, what had previously nauseated me became a source of spiritual and physical consolation for me. After that I did not wait long before leaving the world."[22] His way of "leaving the world" involved "going about in the world" with an entirely new set of eyes enlightened by the Gospel vision of Jesus Christ.

For her part, Clare was likewise divinely inspired to join Francis in embracing his way of living the Gospel in the world of Assisi. Of this inspiration she wrote in her own "Testament":

After the most high heavenly Father saw fit in His mercy and grace to enlighten my heart to do penance according to the example and teaching of our most blessed Father Francis, shortly after his own conversion, I, together with the few sisters whom the Lord had given me soon after my conversion, voluntarily promised him obedience, since the Lord had given us the Light of His grace through his holy life and teaching.[23]

While Francis would feel himself energized by God to go about the world in a way as prophet, Clare on the other hand lived out the dimension of prophecy as critique of the social clerical order as she struggled against the papal and patriarchal forces that refused to sanction her way of life and grant her the "privilege of poverty" — the ability for her community to voluntarily embrace poverty as had been granted the men.

Beginning with the Jewish prophets, culminating in Jesus Christ himself, and continuing in the apostles and our own founders, to embrace the divinely ordered invitation is to live in the world under the power of God, despite all powers and principalities to the contrary.

Preaching God's Holiness and the Need for Societal Conversion Promises Rejection by Those Made Apathetic by Its Imperial/Infallible Consciousness (Isa. 6:9–13a)

Upon accepting his divine mission, Isaiah was — perhaps surprisingly — told that nobody would listen and that he would be a failure. The force that had enfleshed God's word in him said:

> Go and say to this people:
>
> > Keep listening, but do not comprehend;
> > keep looking, but do not understand.
> > Make the mind of this people dull,
> >   and stop their ears,
> >   and shut their eyes,
> > so that they may not look with their eyes,
> >   and listen with their ears,
> > and comprehend with their minds,
> >   and turn and be healed. (Isa. 6:9–10)

This particular passage about those who see but do not understand and listen but do not comprehend, lest they understand in their hearts and turn and be converted, is the only one in the whole Hebrew Bible quoted in all four Gospels. As Isaiah's vocation prefigured that of Jesus, so his prophetic call must echo in our hearts individually and corporately as Christians standing in the larger tradition of Jewish prophecy. Such a vocation we are told, by Isaiah and in the Gospels, can be exercised only in the midst of the hardness of heart that is always found in the dominant culture. What Abraham Heschel writes about the context for Isaiah's call, which Jesus also had to face, applies equally to us: "The haunting words which reached Isaiah seem not only to contain the intention to inflict insensitivity, but also to declare that the people already are afflicted by a lack of sensitivity. The punishment of spiritual deprivation will be but an intensification or an extension of what they themselves had done to their own souls."[24]

It is abundantly clear from their narration of Jesus' ongoing struggles with the religious leaders of his day — those connected to the imperial palace and, especially, the untouchable scribes and pharisees — that they were incapable of conversion: in the case of the imperial powers because they thought their way blessed by the imperial gods and in the case of the Jewish leaders because they considered themselves cloaked with a divine mandate of infallibility. They each, respectively, had been coopted by the dominant consciousness and seduced by the ideology of the political economy and the idolatry of a religion gone astray.

Closer to our day the bishops of the Catholic Church in 1971 made a profoundly prophetic statement in the spirit of Isaiah when they commented on the "signs of the times" of that period of history and acknowledged that they needed to be converted to bring about God's plan for the world. Even though they made their statement vis-à-vis the "network" of domination that stifled freedom and kept the greater part of humanity from sharing in the earth's resources, nowhere in any official church document do we find the bishops or officials in the Vatican acknowledging the need for conversion vis-à-vis their exercise of power and its limitation only to those who are celibate males in the church. Despite this selective understanding of their need for conversion, they are very clear about the obstacles to conversion found in societies defined by the dominant consciousness.

In the sexist language of 1971, they said that the schools and the media "which are often obstructed by the established order, allow the formation only of the man desired by that order, that is to say, man in its image, not a new man but a copy of man as he is."[25] With our public schools and media uncritically supportive of the political economy and our Catholic schools and media often attended not so much for their excellence as for their ability to produce students faithful to the institutional magisterium, the bishops' words in 1971 were quite insightful.

But the bishops did not stop there. Recognizing how the dominant consciousness, maintained through education and the media, can be highly resistant to change, they concluded that the only hope for any change in consciousness would come with a radical conversion based on an entirely new kind of education. They say that

> education demands a renewal of heart, a renewal based on the recognition of sin in its individual and social manifestations. It will also inculcate a truly and entirely human way of life in justice, love and simplicity. It will likewise awaken a critical sense, which will lead us to reflect on the society in which we live and on its values; it will make men ready to renounce these values when they cease to promote justice for all men.[26]

The bishops tell us that the purpose of all education is fundamentally a conversion of heart, a transformation of our ways of thinking, and in particular a change in the morals that have justified a pattern of living. Experiencing the message, we embrace it; embracing the message, we become its messengers. Our message encompasses a call to conversion of hearts at all levels — individual, communal, and collective, especially in those structures of injustice whose imperial consciousness and self-proclaimed infallibility will not admit even a need for conversion.

As we proclaim this call to conversion, however, I believe a good dose of compassion will help us, recollecting at all times how we ourselves have been victims of our own ideologies. After all, Isaiah himself was a holy person; yet it wasn't until he was in the "house" that he had the experience of what God's holiness truly meant, including the realization of what sin — his sin, in particular — now truly meant.

Faithful to the prophets we should remember, when resisted by the "true believers," that their resistance does not mean they are evil. We should not be surprised that they will call us unpatriotic, anticapitalist, or disloyal to the pope when we dissent and challenge the dominant consciousness. Whereas the establishment honestly sees its ideologies as divinely sanctioned, incontrovertible truths, we see these as forms of idolatry that profane the holiness of God. While we see such ideology and idolatry profaning God's name, the leaders of our political economy believe they are called to convert the whole world to obeisance before the altar of production and consumption. In the case of our religious leaders, they are convinced they are in full possession of the truth, and so it is understandable that they insist we worship a god who wills that only men preside at the altar.

In repeating this quote from Isaiah about blindness and deafness, Matthew's Jesus would comfort those disciples who proclaimed another vision of God's reign: "Blessed are those who are persecuted for righteousness' sake, for theirs is the kingdom of heaven. Blessed are you when people revile you and persecute you and utter all kinds of evil against you falsely on my account. Rejoice and be glad, for your reward is great in heaven, for in the same way they persecuted the prophets who were before you" (Matt. 5:10–12). As Isaiah experienced rejection for his prophetic utterances and as Jesus died because of his, we who accept the yoke of prophecy as religious can expect nothing less. it should not, then, come as a surprise when it occurs.

In his apostolic exhortation on religious life, Pope John Paul II elaborated on its prophetic characteristics, making special note of the religious who died for their faith. He said that these "deserve to be inscribed in the martyrology of the twentieth century." He celebrate the "thousands of them" who were "forced into the catacombs by the persecution of totalitarian regimes or of violent groups, or have been harassed while engaged in missionary activity, in action on behalf of the poor, in assisting the sick and the marginalized" who gave the gift of their lives.[27] As edifying as it is to read the pope's words highlighting the witness of our contemporary martyrs, it is sad that the pope makes no mention of those who, like Isaiah and Jesus, have had to suffer at the hands of their own co-religionists. The names of those who lost their livelihood when they witnessed to the truth in parishes whose pastors were threatened, those who lost a voice when they were silenced by Rome for teaching what it considered subversive to its male-only laws, those banned from dioceses by bishops who caved in to groups threatening reports to their superiors: these names will not be inscribed in the martyrology of the twentieth century. But I believe they are already written in the Book of Life.

Despite Rejection, an Alternative Community Will Serve as the Seed for Implementing the New Vision of God's Holiness (Isa. 6:13:b)

Although Yahweh promised Judah's annihilation to such a degree that, even "if a tenth part remain in it, it will be burned again, like a terebinth or an oak whose stump remains standing when it is felled" (Isa. 6:13a), this same God also promised that, despite this annihilation, there would be a new, enlivened community that would arise from its decimation: "The holy seed is its stump" (Isa. 6:13b). This seed will be the new family, an alternative household, following the demise of *oikonomía* and *ekklēsía*, which formerly held people's allegiance.

In a world where the family has been undermined, religious life as a new kind of family can provide a special, countercultural meaning, especially if celibacy is lived as a healthy, life-giving alternative to society's promiscuous ways. In the words of Sandra Schneiders, a key way religious offer the witness of a healthy family is precisely in their celibacy: "The free choice of celibacy by Religious is the assumption of a particular stance in regard to sexuality, relationships, and especially the family." She asks: "What does this choice have to contribute to the Christian struggle in this area? I think," she continues, "that if Religious reflect deeply on their choice of consecrated celibacy in light of the Gospel they will indeed discover the prophetic valence of their vocation for this turbulent and critical area" of what it means today to be "family."[28]

I have already stressed the need for communities formed by alternative consciousness so that members of these communities can support each other in a critique of the dominant culture and its consciousness. Being in solidarity with people who are poor in society and marginalized in the church, members of these alternative communities, these new families, can allow their experience of oppression to move them to even deeper forms of compassion, to promote justice for those who are oppressed and conversion of the oppressors so that, in truth, Jesus' vision of God's reign may become good news to the poor.

When I was in Brazil for the Fifth Plenary Council of my Capuchin Franciscan order (1986), we gathered around the theme of "Our Prophetic Presence in the World." Having personally seen the *favelas* and heard the stories of the *sem terristas* (landless ones), we quoted a passage from Pope Paul's apostolic exhortation more than any other. Noting that we "hear rising up, more pressing than ever, from their personal distress and collective misery, 'the cry of the poor,'" the pope says this cry had such an impact on religious "in so dramatic a fashion that some of you even feel on occasion the temptation to take violent action." Urging them to refrain from such violence and to remember always how Christ responded to the oppressed and victimized of his day, Paul VI offered two ways religious must respond prophetically, if they are to be faithful: "How then will the cry of the poor find an echo in your lives? That cry must, first of all, bar you from whatever would be a compromise with any form of social injustice. It obliges you also to awaken consciences to the drama of misery and to the demands of social justice made by the Gospel and the Church."[29] The pope continues by declaring that the cry of the poor "leads *some of you* [emphasis added] to join the poor in their situation and to share their bitter cares."[30]

The only groups where I have found Pope Paul VI's call for a prophetic renewal of religious life being implemented is in some alternative communities, often functioning within a wider religious context that has been created to sustain these smaller groups in their vision. An example is the Grand Rapids Dominicans who have continually challenged the military-industrial complex, with the support of the wider congregation — not to mention that it is one of those few institutions committed to paying just salaries to their employees in the form of a sustainable living wage.

With Patricia Wittberg, I personally believe such communities need to be "intentional" rather than "associational,"[31] group-defined rather than personally ordered, and congregated regularly (even daily) rather than periodically gathered. By promoting such communities, I may receive opposition. Indeed any who promote a notion of community that includes geographic location can expect strong reaction, but I think this is because most still are locked into an understanding of religious life reflective of the past forty years since Vatican II rather than living as religious through the lens of a prophetic call.

One of the first things the Jewish prophets did, as already noted, was to create schools of disciples; a *nâbî* formed *nâbîim*. We do not know the kind of support system such communities then entailed, but such relationships were not only necessary that the prophetic message be echoed in others; I believe they were strategic insofar as they helped empower the prophet to continue proclaiming the message to the priests and the kings.

Today we need to have regular and ongoing support if we are to be prophetic. Such support demands that we develop new forms of religious life based on the assumption that all members are seeking the face of God in contemplation to deepen the mystical life; that they are affirming and challenging each other in conversation as the prophetic proclamation is discerned; and that they are finding ways of supporting each other in their celibacy by developing deep friendship, mutuality, intimacy, and trust. Because I indeed live in such a community, I cannot imagine how a truly prophetic stance could be maintained without a common life ordered to witness to the prophetic.

No matter what form these new communities take, women and men religious must constitute themselves as liminal groups, subcommunities of resistance, as described by Walter Brueggemann. Such a subcommunity, he notes, is likely to be ones in which

- there is a *long and available memory* that sinks the present gen-eration deep into an identifiable past that is available in song and story;

- there is an available, expressed *sense of pain* that is owned and recited as a real social fact, that is visibly acknowledged in a public way, and that is understood as unbearable for the long term;

- there is an *active practice of hope,* a community that knows about promises yet to be kept, promises that stand in judgment on the present;

- there is an *effective mode of discourse* that is cherished across the generations, that is taken as distinctive, and that is richly coded in ways that only insiders can know.

In short, such a subcommunity is one in which the first-line, elemen-tal realities of human, bodily, historical existence are appreciated, honored, and treasured. It is obvious that such a subcommunity knows itself to be positioned for the long term in tension with the dominant community that responds to the subcommunity at best as an inconvenience, at worst as an unbearable interruption.[32]

With Brueggemann's required elements needed to ensure a prophetic subcommunity, it can be assumed that, among existing religious communities, their existence will be few and far between, and none of us should be surprised. As I said earlier, given the external obstacles from church and society and the internal resistance from those who entered religious life under another set of expectations, the only viable way for a religious community to adopt such a prophetic stance will be by its members committing themselves intentionally, with mutual accountability as the new form of obedience, to the fulfillment of Paul VI's vision. It is not enough to have communities with prophetic "refounders"; we must refound our communities themselves as prophetic.

Moses might have dreamed of a world where "all the Lord's people were prophets, and that the Lord would put his spirit on them" (Num. 11:29); popes may have said that all religious are called to be prophetic; religious themselves may have echoed this in their various documents. Given the limitations and the vision of Isaiah and its demands, I'll be satisfied with a remnant who don't classify themselves as prophets but who spend their time trying to let happen in their lives the enactment of the mystical/prophetic call that led Isaiah to be the prophetic witness he was in the world of his kings — be they Uzziahs, Jothams, Ahazes, or Hezekiahs. If, in the process of being faithful to their call, they are perceived to be prophets by the people, then they will be prophetic in deed, not just in their pronouncements. Until that happens it will not only be "the people" who will perish for want of such prophecy; religious life itself will perish as a viable form of witness.

Three

Jeremiah and the Scroll:
The Need to Be Formed in the Word

Jeremiah as Transitional Figure between the "Old" and the "New"

Jeremiah is the second prophet I consider a model for what it means for us as religious to give utterance to the prophetic in church and society today. In some ways the context for his prophecy might be considered comparable to the situation of the majority of religious in the developed nations today, in that Jeremiah's ministry took place mainly in Judah's era of prosperity and power. He also therefore represents all of us who are reluctant to accept our role of challenging empire and *ekklēsía.*

According to Abraham Heschel, a prophet's "essential task is to declare the word of God to the here and now."[1] Building on Heschel's insight, Franciscan sister Mary C. Carroll notes specifically of Jeremiah in his historical context, his "then and there," as it were, that he "had to break Judah's addiction to other gods, prepare hearts with searing words, and be an effective mediator. . . . Might we be in a similar situation, with questionable values seeping into our consciousness, making personal and ecclesial purification more urgent?"[2] If it is purification we all need, personally, communally, and collectively, then we religious might learn a lesson from Jeremiah, for everything in Jeremiah's vocation emanated from the way God's word found its home in his heart. Witnessing to that word in his heart became a work of love. The word became the spark of the divine in him. His response revealed the spark as a flame of fire.

Jeremiah's story begins by setting forth the historical context for his vocation, noting the various rulers beginning with King Josiah and ending with Jerusalem's captivity (Jer. 1:1–3), at which point we then read how "the word" of God came to him, in a way, I daresay, many religious can understand.

Now the word of the Lord came to me saying,

> "Before I formed you in the womb I knew you,
> and before you were born I consecrated you;
> I appointed you a prophet to the nations."

Then I said, "Ah, Lord God! Truly I do not know how to speak, for I am only a boy." But the Lord said to me,

> "Do not say, 'I am only a boy';
> for you shall go to all to whom I send you,
> and you shall speak whatever I command you.
> Do not be afraid of them,
> for I am with you to deliver you, says the Lord."

Then the Lord put out his hand and touched my mouth; and the Lord said to me,

> "Now I have put my words in your mouth.
> See, today I appoint you over nations and over kingdoms,
> To pluck up and to pull down,
> to destroy and to overthrow,
> to build and to plant. (Jer: 1:4–10)

This bonding was an invitation to intimacy in the depth of his soul. Reflecting on this passage Meister Eckhart, the Dominican mystic, wrote:

The prophet says: "He has stretched forth his hand" (Jer. 1:9). And he means by that the Holy Spirit. Now he goes on to say: "He has touched my mouth" and means by this that "God has spoken to me" (Jer. 1:9). The mouth of the soul is the highest part of the soul and this is meant by saying "God has put his word in my mouth" (Jer. 1:9). That is the kiss of the soul: there mouth comes to mouth; there the Father gives birth to the Son in the soul, and there is where the soul is addressed."[3]

Addressed in his soul, Jeremiah was to address the nations (1:5, 9). Formed in the word, he must proclaim that word. Jeremiah's vocation, like that of the other prophets we are considering (see Isa. 6:6ff.; Ezek. 3:1ff.), can never be exercised apart from mission. His call did not come for his personal edification but for his compatriots and all of creation. His response arose from a willingness on his part to be open to conversion, expressed in a selfless, all-embracing witnessing to the word he felt burning within him. Likewise, I believe, only when we religious feel the same power of God's word in us will we be able to recapture our call and make it relevant for our times.

Perhaps in the word "witness" we best discover the meaning of the call of a prophet like Jeremiah. As we noted in the last chapter, prophets don't serve history only as mouthpieces of God; they who have experienced God's word in the depths of their being intuit the nature and identity of God. From this they keenly grasp God's agenda for themselves and their people. They become the moralists of nations, the conscience of peoples, the arbiters of God's will in the universe. Jeremiah called this will of God "God's plan," and, upon receiving his call, Jeremiah spent the rest of his life witnessing to God's word and plan for the people.

Jeremiah's experience of being overpowered by God's word in the depths of his being in contrast to the desensitization and false consciousness of his people created within him an anger born of grief. That anger was so visceral, voluminous, and vocal that, even today, we call strong outbursts "jeremiads." However, unlike today's "jeremiad," which usually is expressed in calling down fire and brimstone on those who won't do what *we want*, Jeremiah's "jeremiad" reflected instead what Heschel calls the pathos of God; a protest against a people insistent on doing what *God did not want*.

Jeremiah's jeremiad was uttered against those who violated God's plan of justice and mercy. In a culture of apathy, Jeremiah's empathy reflected God's pathos in a marked way. As such, Heschel has written, Jeremiah stands out as an exemplar of all that is prophetic:

The prophet is no hireling who performs his duty in the employ of the Lord. The usual descriptions or definitions of prophecy fade to insignificance when applied, for example, to Jeremiah. "A religious experience," "communion with God," "a perception of His voice" — such terms hardly convey what happened to his soul: the overwhelming impact of the divine pathos upon his mind and heart, completely involving and gripping his personality in its depths, and the unrelieved distress which sprang from his intimate involvement.[4]

For those of us trying to allow God's word to ground us in God's pathos, our call to identify with prophets like Jeremiah demands that we become women and men passionate about God's word. We need to get a little of the fire of God's anger in our hearts, as Jeremiah did, and speak to the hardness of hearts in the world around us. Walter Brueggemann puts Jeremiah forward as "as the clearest model for prophetic imagination and ministry. He is a paradigm for those who address the numb and denying posture of people."[5] Jeremiah rightly stands as a model for those of us who are reluctant prophets and resistant pilgrims.

The Witness of Jeremiah: To Be without Wife or Children

A critical element of Jeremiah's witness to God's fecundity and love was the demand that he witness to Israel's and Judah's barrenness and infidelity in his own body. This specific witness was that he remain without a wife and be without children (Jer. 16:2ff). As such Jeremiah's call to celibacy stood not as a blessing in his life but as a protest about his people's living; not as a consecration of his body but a condemnation of the body politic of his people. Such an insight might help clarify some of the present-day confusion about whether celibacy stands as a mandate that can be legislated by humans or if celibacy is a gift in the church. Just as Jeremiah's celibacy was to stand as a witness to reinforce his mission, so our mission — of proclaiming God's reign to empire and *ekklēsía* — demonstrates that the charism of religious life is bigger than but inclusive of its celibate expression.

This attitude toward celibacy is especially important as the overall numbers in the developed world of those willing to be celibate become fewer compared to times past. For this reason, I believe, the charism of prophecy itself can never be identified with the charism of celibacy; the two totally differ as "gifts" given by the Spirit to the church. Indeed, being celibate is not essential to the prophetic life at all. Otherwise why would Isaiah be told to have three sons? In his case not being celibate, but fecund, attested best to God's plan for the people.

If we examine the contemporary charism of prophecy as it has been expressed in the great founders of religious orders, such as Benedict of Nursia and Francis of Assisi, Angela Merici and Catherine MacAuley, we find the expression of this gift to the wider church has never been limited to its celibate expression and indeed has often encompassed the laity. Thus, those granted the prophetic charism could be married, widowed, or single in our own tradition. Given this notion of the charism constituting a call and mission for the wider church, one might argue that, indeed, if the charism of such founders would not be able to find expression beyond a celibate witness, its gift to the wider church would be compromised. An awareness of this unrestricted action of the Spirit becomes especially important as vocations to the celibate expression of the charism are diminishing at the same time as large numbers of laypeople, single and married, want to become our "associates."

However, Jeremiah was called to celibacy, and his specific witness was meant to serve as a symbolic protest against the infidelity of his people. In this light, therefore, I hold that unless our call to celibacy is manifested as part of the deeper dimension of prophetic protest, our celibacy will not likely be either healthy or countercultural. As I look at the dominant consciousness, I find great reason to use celibacy as a protest: against the pornographic, narcissistic, abusive, violent, and manipulative forms of sexual exploitation. But, on the other hand, when I consider how celibacy has come to be an ecclesiastical demand of two groups of people in our church — priests and homosexual people — the value of celibacy freely embraced as part of a divine call unmasks the demand for celibacy not as a prophetic protest but rather as a form of asserting power and control over these two groups — the very antithesis of God's purpose in Jeremiah..

We who are celibate must find a place for God in the center of our lives from which all warmth and intimacy will flow, to be healthy as celibates we would do well to consider celibacy from the perspective of Jeremiah's vocation: as a kind of fasting that is simultaneously fasting *from,* fasting *for,* and fasting *with.*[6] To simply "fast from" genital expression in adherence to a law will simply make us sexual anorexics. Jeremiah's celibacy was meant to serve as a repudiation of Judah's ways, to bear witness to the barrenness of his people before the fecundity of God, to grieve for what might have been, as well as a sign of resistance to what had come to pass. Clearly Jeremiah's celibacy was not meant to elicit wonder and emulation but rather discomfort, perhaps even horror. This negative symbol value becomes evident when he was told that he was to be without wife and child and proclaim the destruction that was due his people because of their infidelity:

> And when you tell this people all these words, and they say to you, "Why has the Lord pronounced all this great evil against us? What is our iniquity? What is the sin that we have committed against the Lord our God?" then you shall say to them: It is because your ancestors have forsaken me ... and because you have behaved worse than your ancestors, for here you are, every one of you, following your stubborn evil will, refusing to listen to me (Jer. 16:10–12).

The people's infidelity was expressed in the way they had been se-duced by powers that were not God. "They polluted my land with the carcasses of their detestable idols, and have filled my inheritance with their abominations" (Jer. 16:18).

The Difficulty of Challenging One's Own People and One's Co-Religionists

Heschel writes of Jeremiah: "This, indeed, was at the root of his anguish. Those whom he loved he was called upon to condemn."[7] The wound of his people was carried in his heart (Jer. 8:18), but the only way he knew this wound could be healed would be to challenge them to change. Because his co-religionists were convinced their "god" to be true, they found it virtually impossible to believe him when he asserted their worship to be of false gods. Despite their religiosity, their hearts were not with the true God. Atheistic in practice, they had come to believe the delusion that their lives were holy, and as a consequence Jeremiah found himself reviled and rejected when he demanded another way to live.

Likewise, those who speak against the virtual atheism of our own times will find themselves alienated and misunderstood, persecuted and silenced, and, sometimes, fired or snubbed. Often facing poverty themselves, they also may end up like Jeremiah, with only their loincloths to protect them. But, unlike the loincloth of Jeremiah, theirs will not be worn solely as a protest against our society's and our church's infidelity but as a sign of their own fidelity to God's word: "For as the loincloth clings to one's loins, so I made the whole house of Israel and the whole house of Judah cling to me, says the Lord, in order that they might be for me a people, a name, a praise, and a glory. But they would not listen" (Jer. 13:11).

In a message that needs hearing today, Jeremiah made it clear to his co-religionists that, despite God's promises to be with the people forever, this divine promise did not mean that Israel/Judah's territory would be inviolable nor that the institution of the temple would remain forever. Indeed he continually reminded them, even after it was too late, that the territory could and would be abandoned, that the temple could and would be destroyed. At Jeremiah's time as in our own, this possibility of institutional destruction was very difficult for the people to hear. Consequently, they rejected his words on the assumption that their god could not and would not abandon them or their territory or their temple. In response to such hardness of heart, Yahweh said: "They have spoken falsely of the Lord, and have said, 'He will do nothing. No evil will come upon us, and we shall not see sword or famine.' The prophets are nothing but wind, for the word is not in them" (Jer. 5:12–13).

Jeremiah railed against this delusion of indestructibility, and because his denunciation was addressed primarily to the priests and rulers, of religion and the political economy, he found himself exiled. By speaking his truth, Jeremiah became an enemy of the state, and, thus marginalized, his exile began spiritually among his people even before he was literally separated from them in geographic exile.

Jeremiah was sent by God to proclaim to the leaders of the temple, the priests themselves, that they had violated their calling. They "destroyed my vineyard, they have made my pleasant portion a desolate wilderness. They have made it a desolation" (Jer. 12:10–11). This part of his message was the hardest for Jeremiah to preach and the most difficult for his co-religionists, especially the priests, to hear (see Jer. 23:1–7, 33–40; 50:6–7). God's word made the reason abundantly clear: "For from the least to the greatest of them, everyone is greedy for unjust gain; and from prophet to priest, everyone deals falsely. They have treated the wound of my people carelessly, saying, 'Peace, peace,' when there is no peace" (Jer. 6:13–14). Indeed, they would not hear his prophecy — until it was too late.

In many ways, Jeremiah's situation reminds me of the recent situation following Cardinal Law's resignation and the adoption of the norms of the U.S. bishops for pedophile clergy when church leaders thought they and the rest of the church could return "to business as usual,"[8] could continue to exercise their power without outsiders' critique, could ignore the clear word spoken by God in the situation and instead simply pursue their own male, celibate, clerical interests. Jeremiah reminds us that "business as usual," when ordained to sustain a system of sin of exclusion and discrimination, must be put out of business.

Besides being celibate in a manifestly public way (19:1ff; 27:2ff), wearing the loincloth (Jer. 13:1–10), and not marrying or having children, Jeremiah demonstrates three other elements that must give shape to our call as religious if our lives are going to be prophetic in a way that witnesses to God's absolute primacy in our lives and our world: (1) how we are called to allow God's word to penetrate our beings; (2) how we allow the divine pathos to take over our beings; and (3) how, in the face of the evil of societal apathy and ecclesiastical anomie, we constructively direct our anger as a manifestation of God's wrath.

The Call to Allow God's Word to Penetrate Our Beings

God's creative pathos penetrated Jeremiah's heart, and it fashioned him to be a witness to God's plan for his world of Israel. The revelation of God's word speaking within him enabled him to experience the depth of the divine plan for his compatriots. Giving full expression to God's word was not exactly what Jeremiah wanted. Knowing that he would have to witness to God's word among a hard-hearted, righteous people seemed futile and frustrating. And yet, despite his protests to the contrary, Jeremiah allowed God's word to penetrate the core of his being, to pummel him into obedience, and to identify with it in his very person so that its orthodoxy became his orthopraxy.

Originally Jeremiah thought he would be able to keep God's word to himself, but something in him would not allow it. Its power demanded that this divine word be made flesh, not only in his words, but in his very being. Plaintively he declared of God's seductive ways:

> O Lord, you have enticed me,
>   and I was enticed;
> you have overpowered me,
>   and you have prevailed...

> For the word of the Lord has become for me
>   a reproach and derision all day long.
> If I say, "I will not mention him,
>   or speak any more in his name,"
> then within me there is something like a burning fire
>   shut up in my bones;
> I am weary with holding it in,
>   and I cannot (Jer. 20:7–9).

In one of the best-known passages in Jeremiah we are told that the "word came to Jeremiah from the Lord: 'Take a scroll and write on it all the words that I have spoken to you against Israel and Judah and all the nations, from the day I spoke to you, from the days of Josiah until today. It may be that when the house of Judah hears of all the disasters that I intend to do to them, all of them may turn from their evil ways, so that I may forgive their iniquity and their sin'" (Jer. 36:1–3). In other words Nebuchadnezzar was going to come and destroy Judah (Jer. 36:29), a national threat that the people would not embrace easily.

At first, upon hearing this message from the lips of Jeremiah, the people were moved deeply. When the royal court heard about the words contained in the scroll, King Jehoiakim and his cohorts felt called to hear it as well. But since the prophecy critiqued the royal ways, and because the king did not deal with challenges to his regime lightly, he cast the scroll into a fire and ordered Jeremiah to be imprisoned, hoping that, with Jeremiah out of the picture, the prophecy could be forgotten. However, instead of waiting for the king's plan to eliminate him, Jeremiah went into hiding. Not only did he remove himself from the threat; once safe, he wrote the prophecies again to challenge the king anew.

Walter Brueggemann frames the significance of the conflict evoked by the scroll as the tension that exists "between royal power and *scroll power*."[9] He writes: "Jeremiah understood that in some inscrutable way, liberated prophetic imagination and experience take the form of a scroll."[10] In the face of the words coming from the rulers and priests, only such a scroll coming from the power of God would have the force to unmask their words as empty promises and claims. Having been empowered by the word, Jeremiah could not allow its burning in a fire set by a frustrated king to extinguish the flame that had consumed his heart. His commitment to rewrite the words shows that, when the word of God penetrates one's heart, it trumps all human decrees if they do not measure up to the eternal truth revealed by God.

Jesus as Word, Scroll, and Text

In the fullness of time, when God's ultimate truth was revealed, it came as that word called "Christ." Christ broke into human history through God's own incarnation in the form of Jesus' life and his witness of the good news. Jesus Christ became a living scroll, an embodied word that was his very being. All the various human words from Jesus' mouth were merely manifestations of the deeper divine word that came to be known as one word — *euangélion:* "gospel."

In the New Testament *euangélion* has two meanings: the first refers to Jesus' indication of God's reign, as over against any mortal regime; the second expresses the more individualistic notion proffered in the Acts of the Apostles and Paul's writing, which modified the original prophetic and countercultural meaning of "gospel" on behalf of the poor into something much more personally salvific.

When Jesus began his "public ministry" he came proclaiming the "good news" of God's reign. In unrolling the scroll to find in it the word his life would proclaim (see Luke 4:18), he made it clear that he and his followers must find their lives grounded in the word, the scroll, and the text. His preaching of good news was accompanied by his teaching "in their synagogues" and his healing of sickness and disease of all kinds (Matt. 4:23; 9:35). When John the Baptist in prison heard about this preaching, teaching, and healing of Jesus, he sent word by his disciples asking Jesus, "Are you the one who is to come, or are we to wait for another?" (Matt. 11:3). John, who had led a life of austerity and fiery, prophetic preaching, could not at the beginning envision how Jesus' words and deeds met his own predetermined and received criteria for the Messiah. Inviting John to change his way of thinking, Jesus pointed to the reordering of relationships that was taking place in his own life and ministry: the blind now saw, the lame could walk, lepers were being cleansed, deaf people could hear, and dead people were coming alive. In concluding that "the poor have good news brought to them," he declared: "And blessed is anyone who takes no offense at me" (Matt. 11:6). In other words, the good news that is given to the poor is a gospel that stands opposed to that of any empire.

Another of the infrequent more prophetic uses of the word *euangélion* occurs in the story of a woman who, toward the end of Jesus' life, "came to him with the alabaster jar of very costly ointment" and poured it on his head while he was "in the house" (Matt. 26:1), Jesus said that her action of reordering her resources in that house (*oikía*) modeled true discipleship forever and for all: "Wherever this good news is proclaimed in the whole world, what she has done will be told in remembrance of her" (Matt. 26:13).

In a world where Jesus also said, "You always have the poor with you" (Matt. 26:11), what did *she do* that merited Jesus' proclamation about her and how she must be remembered among his disciples? The good news Jesus proclaimed and to which the woman witnessed cannot be understood except in the context of the imperial reality in which these words and deeds occurred. In those days "good news" was actually a technical phrase used by the Romans when the emperor won another victory, which meant the empire would be extended in space. Other times "good news" meant the announcement that the emperor had been given a male child, involving a similar extension of the imperial dynasty, in this case in time. In both cases the proclamation of "good news" meant the insurance or security of the empire either over its enemies or in its heirs in place and time.

Such a culturally accepted proclamation of the "good news" thus indicated that an empire based on injustice would be sustained in the here (place) and now (time). So when Jesus proclaimed another "good news," asserting a very different reign of justice that he came to fulfill (Matt. 3:15), his manifesto was meant to subvert the whole imperial apparatus. Moving to the religious sphere, his gospel about fulfilling all justice (Matt. 3:15) could not be limited to proclamatory words; the "gospel" had to be expressed in a way that would exceed the kind of "justice" promoted by the religious leaders. Baptized into the way of justice (Matt. 3:15), he demanded that his followers' justice exceed that of the religious leaders as well (Matt. 5:20). Such a gospel could only get him and any others who embraced it into trouble with both his culture and its cultic supporters. Thus Walter Brueggemann writes:

Jesus came to those paralyzed by the demands of the overpunctilious requirements of some forms of Judaism that had been diverted from the claims of God and neighbor, and by the comprehensive ideology of the Roman government that wanted to eliminate the God of the Jews from its horizon. As the story goes, Jesus came among those frozen in narratives of anxiety and alienation, of slavery and fear; he authorized a departure into the new world of God's governance. He appeared abruptly, and he said, "Repent-turn-change-switch, for the new governance is at hand."[11]

Jesus said that those who would follow his way of wholeness would have to reorder their lives on behalf of the poor (Matt. 19:21). Without a doubt, Jesus' proclaiming "good news" involved a gospel that was specifically oriented to a social agenda: to make sure that the poor would have justice served on their behalf. This alone constituted "doing good." The woman with the wealth could "do good"; the rich young man could not (see Matt. 19:16ff). Such was the demand for conversion contained in Jesus' proclamation of the "good news."

After Jesus died and rose, the prophetic "good news" became more individualized, with a second meaning of *euangélion* taking over. Those who proclaimed the "good news" in the streets and synagogues interpreted it to mean Jesus' passion and death, resurrection and Pentecost insofar as this enabled those who would identify with him to possess within themselves and among themselves the living presence of the Spirit of Christ (see Acts 8:12, 35; 13:32; 14:15; Rom. 10:145; 1 Thess. 3:6; 1 Pet. 1:12).

The prophetic call to social and ecclesiastical transformation was lost in the new meaning. Thus, in one short generation of preaching, the good news of God's reign that Jesus proclaimed — which had such imperial and religious implications that it resulted in the society's leaders conspiring to kill him — was eclipsed by the good news of Jesus' death and resurrection and its empowerment of those who would believe in him as their savior. The original political and subversive gospel became personally salvific good news. The call to social transformation was muted by the stress on individual conversion.

At the beginning of his ministry, before Jesus began proclaiming the good news of God's reign in the midst of the imperial dynasty (Matt. 4:23), he was "led up by the spirit into the wilderness to be tempted by the devil" (Matt. 4:1). The wilderness was the place of testing regarding the way Jesus would choose to address life's basic needs: power, possessions, and prestige. In this arena Jesus had to decide if he would embrace the "good news" of the imperial and religious leaders of his day or proclaim another kind of good news that would usher in the reign of God.

The wilderness represented what today would be called "exile." In the wilderness, as an exile, Jesus had to choose whether he would deal with power, possessions, and prestige according to the pattern dominant in his wider society, which was under the domain of the devil (Matt. 4:9), or embrace an alternative way of ordering wealth in all its expressions. There he had to decide whether he would succumb to the ideology of his world and its leaders or become, as Edward W. Said says of contemporary exiles, one of "the nay-sayers, the individuals at odds with their society and therefore outsiders and exiles in so far as privileges, power, and honors are concerned."[12]

The original political and subversive gospel became personally salvific good news. The call to social transformation was muted by the stress on individual conversion.

To each of the temptations offered him, Jesus countered with a passage from Deuteronomy written about the years when Israel was in its own desert awaiting the good news of entrance into a promised land. By using the Deuteronomy passages, Walter Brueggemann writes, Jesus' threefold riposte to the devil's challenge showed that Jesus, like Jeremiah, was a person "of the scroll." As he was tempted to embrace the ideology of the dominant imperial and religious culture, he rejected it because his baptism demanded the proclamation of another word: the justice that would be expressed in a new kind of baptism at the heart of all creation (Matt. 3:15).

Noting the challenge for us to become people of the word, the text, and the scroll, Walter Brueggemann has written: "Jer. 36, along with

Matt. 4, . . . attests to the danger and power of being a texted people."
And if we are to become liminal subcommunities we must do so by letting
the word become paramount in our lives.

Brueggemann gives us the outline of how we are to become a people
of the "scroll." This involves three steps: (1) a commitment on the part
of the members to become a people of the text (we religious do this by
our vow formulary); (2) an understanding that becoming people of the
text demands that we follow Jesus by continually standing in the imperial
reality under his "good news" (which means we must continually read the
signs of the times in light of the alternative vision of the Gospel) in a way
(3) that this "good news to the poor" is proclaimed by us as a "great and
relentless enemy of silence"[13] (which means we cannot be seduced into
submission by appeals to patriotism toward the empire or loyalty toward
the papacy when such no longer are at the service of the Gospel).

Francis's Experience of the Word

Two passages from Thomas of Celano, the first biographer of Francis of
Assisi, involve Francis's embrace of the word he heard echoing in his heart
in a way that gave him ultimate meaning for his life. Like Jeremiah when
he found God's words, he ate them so that they became to him "a joy
and the delight of my heart" (Jer. 15:16). Once Francis understood how
God's word was leading him into the way of good news, he joyfully and
delightedly proclaimed: "This is what I want with all my heart." However,
unlike Jeremiah — who had so many bad days that he rued the day God
created him and empowered him in the living word (Jer. 4:19; 20:7–18;
23:9) — Francis found in God's word a source of deep consolation and
comfort, even in the most distressing times.

In the first passage about Francis's embrace of the word, Celano describes what we have been calling the ideology of the dominant culture
and the subtle ways it numbs us all psychically and spiritually: "a deadly
disease [that] had grown up everywhere to such a extent and had so taken
hold of all the limbs of many that, were the physician to delay even a little,
it would snatch away life shutting off the life-giving spirit."[14] In commenting on Francis's espousals to the One surpassing even the gods of religion,
Celano writes: "Indeed, the immaculate spouse of God is the true religion
which he embraced; and the hidden treasure is the kingdom of heaven,

which he sought with such great desire; for it was extremely necessary that the Gospel calling be fulfilled in him who was to be the minister of the Gospel in faith and in truth."[15] In other words, Francis had to become a living sign of the word, the scroll, and the text. He had to become a man of the gospel.

The second passage describes a powerful event at the end of Francis's life of trying to let "the Gospel calling be fulfilled in him." Celano writes:

> When Francis was ill and filled throughout with pains, his companion once said: "Father, you have always sought refuge in the Scriptures, and they have always given you remedies for your pains. I pray you to have something read to you now from the prophets; perhaps your spirit will rejoice in the Lord." The saint said to him: "It is good to read the testimonies of Scripture; it is good to seek the Lord our God in them. As for me, however, I have already made so much of Scripture my own that I have more than enough to meditate on and revolve in my mind. I need no more, son; I know Christ, the poor crucified one.[16]

As Celano interpreted it, Francis's joyful embrace of the gospel became a model of conversion to everyone. As one of those, I believe everyone needs to reclaim the gospel in ways that will allow the word to become grounded in us and produce a rich harvest of good news to the poor.

When we of the Franciscan family examine our various vow formulas, we see that in one way or another we actually vow ourselves to a certain "form of life": namely, the gospel. This vow formula is merely the personalization of a deeper formula called the Franciscan form of life. Thus, the opening words of the Rule and Life of the Brothers and Sisters of the Third Order Regular of St. Francis declares:

> The form of life of the Brothers and Sisters of the Third Order Regular of Saint Francis is this: to observe the holy Gospel of our Lord Jesus Christ, living in obedience, in poverty and in chastity. Following Jesus Christ after the example of Blessed Francis, let them recognize that they are called to make greater efforts in their observance of the precepts and counsels of our Lord Jesus Christ.[17]

I entered the Capuchin Franciscans to commit myself to "live the Gospel of our Lord, Jesus Christ" as my form of life, and I have been trying to live out this vow, with some success and many stumblings, ever since that day in 1959 when I took on this form of life. t has been my *call*.

As Franciscans we vow to be faithful to the Word of God, and we do this in the Roman Church as part of a rich tradition. Unfortunately I think that we have become burdened by our tradition at times at the expense of the Gospel itself. As a result, I often think Jesus' challenge to the scribes and Pharisees might well be addressed to us: "And why do you break the commandment of God for the sake of your tradition" and, even more condemnatory: "So, for the sake of your tradition, you make void the word of God" (Matt. 10:3, 6).

Given an overconcentration on tradition that has eclipsed the word to such a degree that we, in effect, have scorned it (see Jer. 6:10),[18] I believe it's time that we — Franciscans and all religious — become people of the scroll, that we recommit ourselves to the "good news" of Jesus in both its forms: as a challenge to the prevailing ideology and as a way of personal conversion.

If we are to become people of the scroll, we no longer can remain people of the lie that constitutes the heart of some of the dynamics in the culture that surrounds us. In the section of *Vita Consecrata* where he discusses the need for "Prophetic Witness in the Face of Great Challenges," Pope John Paul II writes:

> The word of God is the first source of all Christian spirituality. It gives rise to a personal relationship with the living God. . . . It is therefore of great benefit for consecrated persons to meditate regularly on the Gospel texts and the New Testament writings. . . . Meditation on the Bible *in common* is of great value. When practiced according to the possibilities and circumstances of life in community, this meditation leads to a joyful sharing of the riches drawn from the word of God, thanks to which brothers or sisters grow together and help one another to make progress in the spiritual life. Indeed, it would be helpful if this practice were also encouraged among other members of the People of God, priests and laity alike.[19]

Listening to the word and remaining in its power will enable us to "have the scriptures fulfilled in our hearing." Fidelity to this text in the context of our time demands another kind of "good news" than that currently proclaimed. Again, I believed, it enhanced in community.

Allowing the Divine Pathos to Capture Our Beings

As we have learned from Jeremiah, Jesus, and Francis, when we embrace the word we cannot be silent. Its power burning in our hearts compels us to unroll the scroll, proclaim its word, and use the text to challenge our context. At the heart of this fire within us is what Heschel calls the "divine pathos." On the one hand this fire represents that which destroys (Jer. 21:14; 43:12; 48:45; 49:27; 50:32); on the other hand, it expresses God's burning anger in the face of human infidelity (Jer. 4:4; 17:4; 21:12). Heschel writes that "the divine pathos is not an absolute force which exists regardless of man, something ultimate or eternal. It is rather a reaction to human history, an attitude called forth by man's conduct; a response, not a cause. Man is in a sense an agent, not only the recipient. It is within his power to evoke either the pathos of love or the pathos of anger."[20]

God's pathos was the heart of the prophetic announcement of "good news." Those who embraced this good news would find God's reign breaking into their world. God's pathos, in other words, would now constitute the center of their world. Heschel writes:

> In sum, the divine pathos is the unity of the eternal and the temporal, of meaning and mystery, of the metaphysical and the historical. It is the real basis of the relation between God and man, of the correlation of Creator and creation, of the dialogue between the Holy One of Israel and His people. The characteristic of the prophets is not foreknowledge of the future, but insight into the present pathos of God.[21]

Jeremiah specifically experienced God's pathos as God's indignation and wrath (6:11) in contrast to the people's apathy and indifference to the injustice among and around them. God's pathos created in him a heart so moved by whatever was alien to God's justice that at times his heart almost broke (23:9). In his own mourning and grieving, sorrow and lament, present in history as well as in nature, Jeremiah's experience of God's pathos was expressed.

Just a cursory glance at the life of Jeremiah shows to what an extent he had experienced this "pathos," as Heschel calls it, this love of God for his people. The a-pathos or apathy of the people, especially those who were the civil and clerical leaders, had created a kind of psychic numbing. Jeremiah, and all the prophets, experienced God's pathos as the antidote to the world's indifference. Because of apathy, the world was numb, and this apathy had to be exposed as an affront to God even if the prophet making the proclamation would be considered an affront to the people.

Despite his sympathy for them and his intercession for the people (15:11), Jeremiah was misunderstood and persecuted by them (15:15). Internal conflicts waged in his heart. At one time he cursed the day of his birth (20:14f); another time he recalls he never wanted his vocation in the first place (17:15–16); at still other times it seems he was almost ready to abandon it (9:2; 15:18ff.; 10:14–18). Yet, despite all the conflicts and all the rejection, he remained faithful. Concerning the model of Jeremiah's ministry, John Bright has written:

> We learn what faith really is: it is not that smug faith which is un-
> troubled by questions because it has never asked any; but that true
> faith which has asked all the questions and received very few an-
> swers, yet has heard the command, Gird up your loins! Do your
> duty! Remember your calling! Cast yourself forward upon God!
>
> In this connection, it would seem, Jeremiah refutes the popular,
> modern notion that the end of religion is an integrated personality,
> freed of its fears, its doubts, and its frustrations. Certainly Jeremiah
> was no integrated personality. It is doubtful if to the end of his tor-
> tured existence he ever knew the meaning of the word "peace." We
> have no evidence that his internal struggle was ever ended, although
> the passing years no doubt brought an increasing acceptance of des-
> tiny. Jeremiah, if his "confessions" are any index, needed a course in
> pastoral psychiatry in the very worst way. No cheap slurs upon the
> function of faith in creating mental and spiritual health, or upon the
> necessary techniques to achieve this end, are, of course, intended.
> Yet the feeling cannot be escaped that if Jeremiah had been inte-
> grated, it would have been at the cost of ceasing to be Jeremiah!
> A man at peace simply could not be a Jeremiah. Spiritual health is
> good; mental assurance is good. But the summons of faith is neither
> to an integrated personality nor to the laying of all questions, but to
> the *dedication* of personality — with all its fears and questions — to
> its duty and destiny under God.[22]

Because of this dedication, this response to the God who calls from within, Jeremiah overcame his fears of persecution and rejection. Despite frustrations and doubts, witnessing to his vocation did bring him some semblance of peace, for he knew it was God's plan that God's word be expressed through him to God's world.

God's Pathos-as-Wrath and Our Empathy-as-Anger toward Societal Apathy

In July 2002 I taught at the Summer Institute of Retreats International at Notre Dame. One night we had an open forum. Those of us who were faculty sat on the stage responding to the concerns and questions from the participants. Though some questions involved the current concerns of the day, the most extended and lively discussion of the evening revolved around the role and future of religious life. Gradually it became a kind of impromptu testimonial to religious life from the many religious in the audience. Overwhelmingly, the women and men speaking, almost all middle-aged or older, said they were happier now in their vocation than they had been at any time previously in their lives.

I rejoiced in their stated happiness, but, to be frank, I could not really identify with the source of their happiness. In almost all cases this "happiness" they spoke of seemed linked to something more individualistic and therapeutic than corporate and beatitudinal. If a life in accordance with the beatitudes is to make us salt of the earth and light to the world, then we, following the prophets, will inevitably be persecuted and misunderstood (see Matt. 5:11–16). I think this is a reason why the experience at Notre Dame that night left me quite uneasy.

My unease stayed with me as I began preparing for the talks to the Neumann/Bachmann group that evolved into this book, and as I reread both the prophets and Abraham Heschel I found out why I was not that happy about their "happiness." In his very first chapter, Heschel makes clear that, instead of being "happy," prophets not only were disheartened vis-à-vis their world; indeed, they might well be called hysterically *un*-happy. Indeed, the prophet often appears to be quite deranged. As we religious find ourselves seduced by imperial ideology and intimidated by appeals to religious infallibility, we would do well to reflect on Heschel's words long and hard. As he describes the prophets' reaction to the dominant consciousness of their day, we should remember that, in our day as well, the very "things that horrified the prophets are even now daily occurrences all over the world." He continues:

> Indeed, the sort of crimes and even the amount of delinquency that fill the prophets of Israel with dismay do not go beyond that which we regard as normal, as typical ingredients of social dynamics. To us a single act of injustice — cheating in business, exploitation of the poor — is slight; to the prophets, a disaster. To us injustice is injurious to the welfare of the people; to the prophets it is a deathblow to existence; to us, an episode; to them, a catastrophe, a threat to the world.
>
> Their breathless impatience with injustice may strike us as hysteria. We ourselves witness continually acts of injustice, manifestations of hypocrisy, falsehood, outrage, misery, but we rarely grow indignant or overly excited. To the prophets even a minor injustice assumes cosmic proportions.[23]

Given their experience of the pathos of the God of the universe, the prophets came to see all life as connected: the individual is the cosmos; the universe is the one. Heschel finds in Jeremiah a classic example of this cosmic dimension of the prophets' empathy by quoting from one of the earliest chapters:

> Be appalled, O heavens, at this,
> Be shocked, be utterly desolate, says the Lord.
> For My people have committed two evils:
> They have forsaken Me,
> The fountain of living waters,
> And hewed out cisterns for themselves,
> Broken cisterns,
> That can hold no water. (Jer. 2:12–13)

Moving on to examine the anger-as-empathy that gave rise to the prophets' emotional outbursts and tirades against kings, priests, and false prophets, Heschel asks:

Is not the vastness of their indignation and the vastness of God's anger in disproportion to its cause? How should one explain such moral and religious excitability, such extreme impetuosity?

It seems incongruous and absurd that because of some minor acts of injustice inflicted on the insignificant, powerless poor, the glorious city of Jerusalem should be destroyed and the whole nation go into exile. Did not the prophet magnify the guilt?

The prophet's words are outbursts of violent emotions. His rebuke is harsh and relentless. But if such deep sensitivity to evil is to be called hysterical, what name should be given to the abysmal indifference to evil which the prophet bewails? . . .

The niggardliness of our moral comprehension, the incapacity to sense the depth of misery caused by our own failures, is a fact which no subterfuge can elude. Our eyes are witness to the callousness and cruelty of man, but our heart tries to obliterate the memories, to calm the nerves, and to silence our conscience.

The prophet is a man who feels fiercely. God has thrust a burden upon his soul, and he is bowed and stunned at man's fierce greed. Frightful is the agony of man; no human voice can convey its full terror. Prophecy is the voice that God has lent to the silent agony, a voice to the plundered poor, to the profaned riches of the world. It is a form of living, a crossing point of God and man. God is raging in the prophet's words.[24]

When I think of God's rage that echoed in the jeremiad coming from the mouths of prophets like Jeremiah, I cannot help but recall another kind of rage that arose from the hearts of so many in response to events of September 11, 2001. What struck me most was how the nation as a whole did not have the "capacity to sense the depth of misery" our U.S. form of global capitalism had created, "the depth of misery caused by our own failures." Our consciences had been seduced by our lifestyle into silence and support. Indeed, from our national response, it appeared that there was *nothing* wrong with us at all.

However, while God's rage invited restoration in the face of such a calamity, our national rage instead demanded retribution. I recall hearing George W. Bush say that the perpetrators wreaked their havoc in an effort to "destroy our lifestyle." I found myself thinking: "You are totally right, but what you and I mean by that phrase is entirely different." I recalled hearing him earlier call some Islamic countries and North Korea the "axis of evil" and couldn't help but think of how they call us "evil" as well.

As it happened I was in New York City on September 11, 2001. Like everyone else with any pathos I was shocked by what happened. But unlike many, I did not find anger or rage rising unrequested from my heart, nor did I find myself calling for retribution and revenge. In fact, as such voices seemed to get louder to the point of becoming a cacophony, I found myself increasingly isolated from their clamor. As the president and others declared that "our lifestyle" was under attack, I found myself agreeing from a totally different perspective and social analysis. However, instead of being led to protect our ways, I found myself wondering why our "lifestyle" was such that people would feel compelled to kill themselves flying into two of its economic icons in New York and its Pentagon in Washington in order to destroy it.

More and more alienated from the pundits and those who sought a response in a violence that would only reinforce more threats to our "lifestyle," I began wondering if I myself had been so committed to so-cial justice and peace that I had become irrelevant to the mainstream and alienated from my people. Instead of sharing their rage, I could only feel a deep, deep sadness. Furthermore I couldn't explain my feeling nor where it came from. I was overwhelmed at the loss of so many lives of both perpetrators and victims. I could not get out of my head what must be going through the hearts of the survivors of the victims. I did know that this pathos was not unconnected to the loss of my dear brother Pat, who had died just one year before on September 11, 2000. And it was the same date in 1973 when the leaders of my nation's political economy, in order to preserve our "lifestyle," were able to overthrow, with even more resultant deaths, the democratically elected leaders of Chile. Whatever the source, I knew I was grieving and I didn't know why it was taking such hold of me.

The first sense of why I was feeling sorrow for the victims and their families, as well as the perpetrators and their loved ones, came two days later. Because I was in midtown Manhattan with its towering buildings and because that September 11 and days following were filled with blue skies, I could see the smoke arising from Ground Zero only when I'd go to the avenues and look downtown. But on September 13 the wind shifted.

As the wind came "uptown," I found my eyes sore, my nose filled up, and my mouth feeling very chalky. I did not know what was happening to me until it dawned on me: it wasn't just that the smoke from Ground Zero was getting into me; I realized what and, especially, who now had come to constitute that smoke. Inside of me were the perpetrators and the victims in a way I never imagined. I realized then, as never before, how connected I was with them and they with me. I was one with them and they were actually part of me. We were one in the divine energy at the heart of the universe.

The next day I became aware of another possible source for my grief. Three days after the planes plowed into the World Trade Center, the Pentagon, and that farm in Pennsylvania, I picked up my breviary for morning prayer, still feeling my alienation from those around me and then discovered the source of my pain.

Week III began with Psalm 51. As I prayed it, I thought it quite applicable to our situation. However, immediately after Psalm 51 the Canticle from Jeremiah spoke directly to the sense of pain I felt. Why were our politicians and corporate leaders unable to question how our activities in the world contributed to the terror we were experiencing? How could the imams remain silent in the face of such destructive actions taken in the name of Allah? Suddenly Jeremiah's insight about his people applied to my own:

> Day and night I weep unending tears,
> for my daughter is struck, my people crushed by a savage blow.
> I see the dead slain in the fields and people starving in the streets.
> Priest and prophet wander about, not knowing where to turn.
> Lord, have you nothing but contempt for Zion?
> Have you completely rejected Judah?
> Why have you inflicted wounds that do not heal?
> We long for peace, we long for healing, but there is only terror.
>   (Jer. 14:17–19; see 4:19)

And after describing the reality of his day with such parallels to our own, Jeremiah concludes with an admission from the lips of his civil leaders:

> We have sinned against you and we know it, God;
> we share our people's guilt. (Jer. 14:20)

Recalling that earlier Jeremiah had warned his people to acknowledge their guilt (Jer. 3:12), I was stunned as I read those words from thousands of years ago. We have yet to hear such a confession from the leaders of our political economy with regard to how our lifestyle has devastated peoples and the planet. We have yet to hear such an act of contrition from bishops, curial officials, and popes about the consequences of becoming an overly patriarchal and clericalized church. Like the leaders of Jeremiah's world, our own leaders have become so indoctrinated in the ideology of imperial ways and infallible truths that they literally are unable to imagine converting to another vision of life. Their psyches have become numb, their hearts have become indifferent, and they see absolutely no reason why they need to change.

Unfortunately, my experience in New York reinforced for me what Walter Brueggemann writes about Jeremiah. He knew "long before the others that the end was coming and that God had had enough of indifferent affluence, cynical oppression, and presumptive religion." His grief was mine, a grief felt in two ways. Brueggemann says:

> First, it was the grief he grieved for the end of his people. And that was genuine grief because he cared about this people and he knew that God cared about this people. But the second dimension of his grief, more intense, was because no one would listen and no one would see what was so transparent to him. So his grief was kept sharp and painful because he had to face regularly the royal consciousness, which insisted "peace, peace" when apparently only he knew there was no peace.[25]

Like Jeremiah I believe that I am witnessing the demise of the soul of my people and the beginning of an exile that we have created for ourselves. Filled with fear and dread on a sustained basis, we will, too late, begin to ask what we may have done to bring us to this point.

In conclusion I am struck by the two kinds of divine pathos that Jeremiah experienced: wrath and indignation on the one hand and love and compassion on the other. For Jeremiah this pathos is described in his lament: "O land, land, land, hear the word of the Lord!" (Jer. 22:29), echoed by Jesus in his own lament over Jerusalem: "Jerusalem, Jerusalem, the city that kills the prophets and stones those who are sent to it! How often have I desired to gather your children together as a hen gathers her brood under her wings, and you were not willing! See, your house is left to you, desolate" (23:37–38).

Sometimes in the face of such apathy, indifference, psychic numbing, anomie, hardness of heart, the only response we have is lamentation. All we can do is grieve — for our nation, our church, our order, our people, ourselves.

We may say we are called to repair the house that is falling into ruins but, as we can see, has become desolate. But just as Isaiah knew that a seed would rise from the stump, so Jeremiah leaves us with an unbelievable promise as well:

> The days are coming, says the Lord, when I will make a new covenant with the house of Israel and the house of Judah. It will not be like the covenant that I made with their ancestors when I took them by the hand to bring them out of the land of Egypt — a covenant that they broke, though I was their husband, says the Lord. But this is the covenant that I will make with the house of Israel after those days, says the Lord: I will put my law within them, and I will write it on their hearts; and I will be their God and they shall be my people. No longer shall they teach one another, or say to each other, "Know the Lord," for they shall all know me, from the least of them to the greatest, says the Lord; for I will forgive their iniquity, and remember their sin no more." (Jer. 31:31–34)

Will this promise be fulfilled in the whole house of Israel and the whole house of Judah, or will it be realized in a remnant? We will probably not live long enough to know the outcome. However, I believe that, whether the community that fulfills the promises in its members will be the whole congregation or, most likely, a liminal subcommunity within it, this outcome will be affected by our choices. The decision, Mary Carroll, S.S.S.F., writes, is up to us:

> Having considered Jeremiah's life and passionate words, our own cultural and ecclesial gods, and the urgency of the more prophetic stance, I hope that we can all be more prophetic than comfortable, more empathically involved than distant, more radically honest than fearfully polite, more full of fire for positive purification than full of criticism for its pain, and more given to realistic hope that to the

platitudes of lip service. I am confident that there will be other, contemporary Jeremiahs, who can remind us and renew us:

> Look, the days are coming, Yahweh declares, when I shall make a new covenant with the house of Israel (and the House of Judah), but not like the covenant I made with their ancestors the day I took them by the hand to bring them out of Egypt, a covenant which they broke, even though I was their Master, Yahweh declares. No, this is the covenant I shall make with the House of Israel when those days have come, Yahweh declares. Within them I shall plant my Law, writing it on their hearts. Then I shall be their God and they will be my people. (Jer. 31:31–34)[26]

Four

Ezekiel as Exile

Ezekiel is the third and last of the major prophets to be considered for our emulation as religious. This priestly member of Jerusalem's elite was called to be "God's strength" — the literal meaning of his name — for a people without bearings, and in their exile his vocation inspired him to offer the people hope.

Ezekiel is the only prophet whose entire ministry took place within the Exile. Whether Ezekiel returned to Israel nobody knows; all that is extant of his prophetic writings encompassed only his Babylonian experience. He was taken into Exile in 587, and his prophecy began when he was thirty, in 593. It continued for a quarter of a century, until he was fifty-five, in 568.

Ezekiel's life as a prophet, like Isaiah's, began with a profound religious experience (Ezek. 1:4–28). From a vision of the four living creatures he felt called to speak to his people who had become a rebellious house (Ezek. 2:5, 7, 8). Like Jeremiah, Ezekiel became a person of the scroll:

> But you, mortal, hear what I say to you; do not be rebellious like that rebellious house; open your mouth and eat what I give you. I looked, and a hand was stretched out to me, and a written scroll was in it. He spread it before me; it had writing on the front and on the back, and written on it were words of lamentation and mourning and woe.
>
> He said to me, O mortal, eat what is offered to you; eat this scroll, and go, speak to the house of Israel. So I opened my mouth, and he gave me the scroll to eat. He said to me, mortal, eat this scroll that I give you and fill your stomach with it. Then I ate it; and in my mouth it was as sweet as honey. (Ezek. 2:8–3:3)

Ezekiel was to absorb the words of the scroll and, in doing so, challenge the powers that controlled Judah. Whether or not they would accept what he said, he could not be hindered. Even though God's word from that scroll might fall on deaf ears and resistant hearts, it would not be silenced.

Before elaborating more fully on the various aspects of Ezekiel's call, message, and commission, it would be good to explore the image of "Babylon," where he found himself exiled during his whole life. "Babylon" conjured up as many territorial images as it contained ideological assumptions. On the one hand it connoted being uprooted violently from one's geographic foundation. The once promised land was lost to the people; their temple, the place identified with God's presence among the people, was destroyed. With territory and temple lost, Judah's political economy as well as its religion collapsed. The devastation could not have been felt more keenly. Ideologically "Babylon" meant that Judah had lost its identity as a people politically, economically, and religiously.

Being a priest, Ezekiel must have felt the loss even more personally. Uprooted from the temple and taken a thousand miles away, he, like so many others, could resonate with the sentiments of Psalm 137, which seems to have been written in that exilic context:

> By the rivers of Babylon —
> > there we sat down and there we wept
> > when we remembered Zion.
> On the willows there
> > we hung up our harps.
> For there our captors
> > asked us for songs,
> and our tormentors asked for mirth, saying,
> > "Sing us one of the songs of Zion!"
> How could we sing the Lord's song
> > in a foreign land?
> If I forget you, O Jerusalem,
> > let my right hand wither!
> Let my tongue cling to the roof of my mouth,
> > if I do not remember you,
> if I do not set Jerusalem
> > above my highest joy. (Ps. 137:1–6)

Current theological trends, particularly those influenced by liberation theology, stress themes related to Exodus rather than whose related to

Exile. In the United States civil religion has long portrayed us as inhabitants of a new land that has enabled us to be free. The Atlantic for us is the Red Sea; George III was the oppressive pharaoh outsmarted by George Washington, our Moses. Appropriating this metaphor every Lent, we Christians too go through our forty days in the desert; every Triduum we celebrate our own Passover. Indeed, Exodus rather than Exile largely sculpts our self-understanding as Catholics living in the United States of America.

Beneath many Exodus images indeed the dream of political or religious liberation exists, but as an image it can unconsciously serve to mask nationalism toward our country and triumphalism in our church as well. Furthermore, being in the richest and most powerful nation in the world, it's a little hard for us to imagine the United States now as poor and oppressed, in need of an "exodus" deliverance. Little wonder, then, that, especially for those of us who are able-bodied, white, male, straight, North American, educated, Roman Catholic priests, the metaphor of Exodus doesn't seem to generate much energy. For these reasons I've begun to consider the "Exile" as a more powerful and appropriate image for the spiritual journey we must take nowadays.[1] It's to this metaphor I now turn.

The Exile was crucial in Israel's life. Indeed, Scripture scholars say the bulk of the Jewish Scriptures, including its understanding of the implications of the Exodus itself, arose directly our of Israel's exilic experience.[2] For key parts of the Jewish Scriptures, the Exile provided a metaphor and paradigm[3] for the spirituality of its audience, a thematic center continued even in the Christian Scriptures. Despite a Gospel like Matthew, in which Jesus is portrayed as a new Moses, Jesus' overall stance toward his world, as well as his preaching, called for a type of self-imposed exile that set him and his followers apart from the dominating dictates of empire and entrenched religion. The other books in the Christian Scriptures also portray the followers of Jesus as a unique group alienated from and facing the collective opposition of the "world." In fact, just as scholars say the Hebrew Scriptures were written from the perspective of Israel's exilic experience, with the biblical scholar Daniel L. Smith we can say: "The entire New Testament is written from the perspective of exile."[4]

The more I experience empire's increasing imperialism and *ekklēsía,* with its intensifying infallibilism, I resonate with the writings of Edward W. Said, a Palestinian. He considered his life to be one of exile. For him exile is "an *alternative* to the mass institutions that dominate modern life."[5] You either "are born into it, or it happens to you." Such, I find, has been the phenomenon that has taken over in me. As I view my life as a U.S. Catholic, I know I have been "born into" these realities, but a deeper awareness of their entrenched ways of sinful control have found me increasingly alienated from them. Said's exile has "happened" to me; with Jesus, I find I have nowhere to lay my head (Matt. 8:20).

In probing the dynamics that took place among the people during the Exile, especially as Ezekiel experienced God at work within the Exile, I've found eight points that might lay the groundwork for a contemporary "Spirituality for Exiles."[6] Reflection and action on these points might help us in our two main prophetic tasks of criticizing and energizing. I offer these eight beacons for reflection under the overall heading that promises us: *"We experience energy in our exile wherever and whenever. . . . "*

Jerusalem's Destruction Invites Us to Experience God's Presence beyond That Mediated by the Temple's Priests

With Judah's def eat, Jerusalem's devastation, and the temple's destruction, the key components of Israel's religious underpinnings vanished. Before, Israel had believed it was God's chosen people, a people set apart, with a complacency born of an understanding that God's eternal covenant meant it would never be abandoned. Now, because it had been unfaithful to its God, another nation under other gods had conquered it. "Robbed of all these elements of her identity," Paul Joyce notes, "it is hardly surprising that profound theological questions were raised in her."[7] Probably its greatest question dealt with Israel's understanding of God and its relationship with this God. Once able to trust who God was and where this God could be found, Israel could no longer trust in the institutions that had been created to sustain its faith. With their demise and destruction, it was inevitable that a religious crisis would occur: either God was not God and, therefore, was false at best or dead at worst, or, if the God of their ancestors and stories was still alive, they would be forced to reorder their theology. Now, if God's historical promises were not to be invalidated, they would have to be interpreted in entirely new ways. Before, rituals performed by priests enabled the people to be in conscious contact with God, to the extent that it eventually seemed that only through the temple priesthood could the people be touched by God's real presence. With the temple destroyed, Ezekiel's vision revealed a God who could not be confined to priesthood or temple, a God whose presence now had to be found in invisible sanctuaries, in the lives and experience of the exiles themselves (Ezek. 1; 11:16).

Many people well-versed in the history of the Catholic Church in the United States have discussed the scandals around priestly pedophilia and episcopal cover-ups in terms that recall for me notions of exile. As with the prophets, whose finger-pointing was directed more at the priests than the people, the same has happened in the United States, with a distinction being made between the bishops as the clerical culprits and the people remaining "the faithful." Thus the liberal priest Richard P. McBrien wrote in his syndicated column: "One of the remarkable aspects of the tragic crisis confronting the Catholic church today is the widespread collapse of support for the hierarchy on the part of a traditionally loyal and dutiful laity."[8] For his part, the neoconservative priest Richard John Neuhaus remarked at what seemed to be the height of the crisis in 2002: "Of course the Church will survive, and more than survive, but I expect this storm is not going to pass any time soon. I except we have not yet seen its full fury. I very much wish that I were more confident than I am that every bishop understands that there can now be no returning to business as usual. The word crisis is much overused, but this is a crisis."[9]

Eugene Kennedy describes well how this happened. Catholic immigrants created powerful institutions with which they identified and powerful leaders to whom they gave uncritical support:

> Catholic priests mediated everything for their immigrant flocks, from paying the rent to organizing unions and filling out their citizenship papers. The people paid them back in the small but true coins of trust, admiration and a protectiveness that gave exempt status to priests in everything from parking tickets to personal foibles. These immigrants, whose women waited on the tables of the wealthy as their husbands patrolled their streets, took great pride in their archbishop's living in a mansion as big as any in Back Bay [Boston].[10]

But now this once-landed church has many of its priests sent into exile, its leaders being increasingly exiled from the people in the pews, even as their voices and behavior are making it clear that the old ways

that engendered uncritical trust will never be seen again. Simply put, the
people no longer believe it can be "business as usual," that the old ways
can be the new ways. Increasingly, in places like once-Catholic Ireland, the
traditional identity and role of the priest have to be totally rethought —
to save the institutional church itself from total irrelevance.

One of the greatest challenges facing us in the Roman Catholic Church,
which has too often boxed the Holy of Holies into clerically controlled
sacramental systems and crumbling institutions, is not just to critique this
limitation to people's experience of the divine. Rather we are challenged
to become witnesses to the holy through *our own* religious experience
grounded in prayer to a trinitarian God. We are called to imagine what
priesthood may mean in its fullest sense when it becomes free of the
abomination of clericalism. We are called to make all things new.

*What makes Catholicism unique is its
sacramental and sacral dimension.*

Despite Ezekiel's frustration with the priests of his religion, Bruce
Vawter and Leslie Hoppe note that "the central emphasis of the Law
for Ezekiel was the reorganization of the priesthood at the head of this
community. The prophet envisaged the restored Israel as a sacral community,"[11] not as one without priests. Indeed priests would have an even
more important role, but he envisioned their functioning as priests in a
vastly different way. In our own case of exile, I envision a church with
priests but without control, and priests defined not by gender or sexual
orientation but by their communion with God and God's people.

What makes Catholicism unique is its sacramental and sacral dimension. I believe we cannot remain truly "Catholic" without these essential
characteristics. In the Exile, Israel never imagined abandoning its Judaic
roots. Rather Ezekiel used the occasion to move his co-religionists to be
purified of its institutions' sinful accretions. In this we can learn from our
ancestors in faith. For instance, Ezekiel's experience of a God beyond the
temple or its house priests invites us to a deeper understanding of the full
implications of the "real presence" based in the baptism of all of us in

Christ. It challenges us to contemplate this manifestation of God-with-us so we can be open to a deeper understanding of the multiple ways the living God is manifest throughout the universe. It calls us to share the fruit of our prayer in structures and rituals that mediate God's "real presence" in inclusive ways, beyond the control of one clerical class.

The anthropologist Mary Douglas has demonstrated that a priestly class's preoccupation with ritual controls with regard to purity and pollution has always arisen in response to danger, especially when a particular group feels threatened.[12] How else can we understand clerical decrees further alienating "priests from people" in the celebration of the Eucharist? When I've talked about the need to celebrate God's presence in new rituals beyond clerical control, some priests have become quite upset and threatened. But this shouldn't be surprising, since they cannot understand a priesthood free of clericalism and its liturgical limits. This clericalism arose out of a need to control; now, as it crumbles, it must be altered freely by our liturgists before even more people abandon the church. We have the opportunity to use our time in exile to create rituals to lead us to encounter the holy in ways not always dependent on ordained priests.

The Boundaries That Limited God's Activity to One Clerical Group Give Way to Those Defined by the Spirit

All people and groups need boundaries so that they can identify themselves as belonging to this group and not another, this nation or that culture in contrast to others. Boundaries, by definition and execution, always involve at least some degree of separation. Until the Exile, the temple in Jerusalem distinguished the sacred from the profane, the Jews from their neighbors, and the priests from the rest of the community. However, once exiled, Israel was forced to develop new boundaries that were not land-based and to express these in rituals free of abomination. In effect, what once was considered sacred had to be found within the profane.

In our exile we will need new boundaries that are more spiritual than institutional, and, while I am not against roles of cleric and lay at liturgy as well as some kind of zero-tolerance for priests who today invade the sexual boundaries of others, I think it is going to take a lot more than new regulations regarding these practices to free our church and society from clerical control and other secularizing influences.

As we find ourselves rejecting classifications based in patriarchy and clericalism, I think we need to ask what kind of boundaries and alternative rituals we will need to create if we actually do prevail in our dreams about a truly inclusive church. In this I was struck by a column in *Commonweal* several years ago. Under the title "Don't Tear Down Fences: First Ask Why They Are There," David R. Carlin Jr. wrote:

> Religions need boundaries. Neglect the boundaries of any church for a few generations, and the church will begin to wither away — a process far advanced among Protestant denominations and visibly underway in American Catholicism.
>
> This is not to say that a church's boundaries should never change; nor is it to say that the church must always utilize the same boundary makers. From time to time there may be good reasons for expanding or contracting boundaries, or for discarding one set of boundary markers and replacing it with another. Boundaries and markers, however, are necessities of organizational life, and woe to the church that forgets this fundamental truth.
>
> While American Catholics in general have tended to forget this fundamental truth during the past thirty years, the most forgetful among them have been "liberal" or "progressive" Catholics, for example, the kind of people who write letters to the editor of *The National Catholic Reporter.* If the average Catholic has adopted a denominational mentality, the liberal Catholic has adopted a hyper-denominational mentality. The former favors a policy that leads to gradual ecclesiastical suicide; the latter a policy tantamount to jumping off a cliff.
>
> Progressives who want to reform the priesthood usually talk about justice, power, and a "priest shortage." These are certainly themes worthy of consideration. But so is the need for boundaries. As long as liberal Catholics remain oblivious to this need, they mustn't be surprised when some people suspect them of not having seriously thought through the consequences of their proposals.
>
> So here's a challenge for the priesthood reformers: Tell us what you have to offer as new boundary markers once we eliminate the all-male, celibate priesthood.[13]

Carlin offers a critical insight and connection that cannot be taken lightly. In this, I hope that elements of what I'm presenting here may offer pointers for such new boundary markers that reflect the trinitarian God.

As we redefine our boundaries, we must resist another temptation of exiles: to have our boundaries defined by dualisms. When this happens we are labeled (and boundaried) with words like "left" and "right" or "conservative" and "progressive." A good example is when many of those on the right are so preoccupied with abortion issues that they are silent on women's rights, or when many of those on the left stress the rights of women in a way that results in silence about the rights of the fetus as a human. Rather than an "either/or" approach, I would hope we might develop a "both/and" style that would be more inclusive than exclusive.

As we extend our commitment to human rights into life beyond the womb, I envision a time when we will insist that women have equal rights with men, that the disabled and able-bodied among us cannot be denied their reproductive rights, that gays and straights have the same rights from conception to death, that the South and the North have mutual rights and responsibilities to help each other in face of need, and that, in our God and in any reality identified with this loving God, there can be absolutely no systemic discrimination, only truth and justice, peace, and compassion.

The Temple's Abomination Arising from Worship of "Man-Made" Images Is Replaced by a Worship Celebrating God's Holiness

One of the most used phrases in Ezekiel refers to God's holiness as revealed to all the nations (Ezek. 20:41; 28:22, 25; 36:23; 38:16, 23; 39:27). Ezekiel's experience of God's holiness, like Isaiah's, grounded him with a moral consciousness that made him deeply sensitive to whatever failed to mirror and measure up to that holiness in his world — be it at the individual, interpersonal, or structural levels. For us this means that the holiness of the trinitarian God in whom all persons are equal in the way they order their relationships and resources now must serve as the energizing force for the creation of new relationships at all levels of life, as well as a critiquing force of anything in any community or collectivity that profanes that holiness. Walter Brueggemann says Ezekiel discerned "the enormous mismatch between the *disinterested holiness* of God and the *utilitarian unrighteousness* of Israel."[14] In Ezekiel's vision, Israel had violated God's holiness with its ritual impurity.[15] He called this idolatry an "abomination." We must be ready to make the same critique.

"Abomination" meant "anything unspeakably offensive to true religion."[16] What Ezekiel castigated as idolatry wasn't just the creation of idols made by human hands but the ideology that lay beneath it, which justified idols as worthy of worship. When people are led to worship false gods, there is something deeper occurring than simple idolatry, or even a violation of a key commandment; it is an abomination. As Brueggemann notes, this abomination did not refer to "any crude sense of wooden or stone images but [is used] in spiritual terms as whatever has alienated this people from its Lord and rendered it inaccessible to God's ordinary communication."[17] The word — and its real meaning — cannot be taken lightly.

Some years ago I attended a lecture by the mathematical cosmologist Brian Swimme. I left his talk awed at the timelessness and expansiveness of this creation and what I considered its source in the continually creating Creator-God. Swimme's insights convinced me even more about the timelessness and expansiveness of our Creator — a good image for us exiles as we sense the lack of boundaries in time and space. But almost immediately another line of thought came to me, eliciting deep rage within me. Articulating the new cosmology, Swimme had invited me to worship in awe a transcendent God continually authoring this universe's story. But the leaders of my church were insisting that I must believe in a tribal god who wills that *he* can be worshiped only with one class of people as priests — the males. They also tell us that it is God's will that this one group of people made in God's image, whose members may be sexually oriented to each other, can show their love to each other no more genitally than those of us who have supposedly freely chosen to be celibates. How can anyone worship so small a god, who places such constraints on just one group of people and who exhibits such class — and crass — arbitrariness?

Ezekiel used the term "prophet" pejoratively for any religious leader of Israel claiming to be or acclaimed to be one who gave voice to the mind of God[18] and who "envisioned falsehood and lying [as] divination" (Ezek. 13:6; see 13:9). As I find more and more contemporary examples of a kind of divination being used to support rules and regulations that now no longer make sense, I wonder what Ezekiel would say of our present religious leaders who insist they divine God's will, who claim it is an infallible truth that God wants husbands and wives to procreate in only one way, only heterosexuals to have sex, and only males to preside at the altar. When an ideology is enshrined as infallible, exile cannot be far away for those who will not be seduced into such a profanation of God's holiness. Bruce Vawter and Leslie Hoppe say that "these prophets, whether in good faith but self-deluded or in bad faith and deliberately deceiving, have professed to speak the mind of the Lord when in reality no spirit other than their own moved them. They have been, he [Ezekiel] says, 'like foxes among ruins.' "[19]

If we don't worship a God who is bigger than our human identifiers for God, our Jerusalems and its temples deserve to be destroyed or, at least, abandoned. Until we understand God's triune holiness and translate it into our structures, we will miss that Spirit-grounded energy promised in Ezekiel's great vision: "I will sprinkle clean water upon you, and you shall be clean from all your uncleanness, and from all your idols I will cleanse you. A new heart I will give you, and a new spirit [*ruah*] I will put within you; and I will remove from your body the heart of stone and give you a heart of flesh. I will put my spirit within you, and make you follow my statues and be careful to observe my ordinances" (Ezek. 36:25–27).

The necessary reorganization of our structures will be impossible, Walter Brueggemann insists, reflecting on the witness of Ezekiel, "if life is reduced to human control. It is precisely this indefatigable power of God's holiness that makes newness possible. My urging, then," he writes in words that make more sense than ever, "is that the holiness of God is a theological theme we do well to recover if there is a will among us for newness. Without this focus on the holiness of God, we are consigned to life as a profaned, flat human enterprise that can only end in despair."[20]

Being Uprooted from What Previously Provided Meaning Is Expressed in Purifying Grief

Like the original Israel, our modern countries in the West were created by willing immigrants. These voluntary expatriates and émigrés, including my own ancestors from Ireland and Germany, displaced long-landed peoples. As I wrote this book, I discovered the undated obituary of my great-great uncle, Peter Murphy. It said he was born May 25, 1851, in the Town of

Mitchell in Sheboygan County, Wisconsin and seemed to brag: "He was the second white child to be born in the Town of Mitchell." This made me wonder, for the first time, who were the ones my ancestors may have exiled as they made their home in this new land. How, in their effort to be free of political and economic domination, might they have created exile for others? What happened to those native peoples that roamed those homesteads in which we once gloried?

Unlike my ancestors who came to this land more or less freely, other people come to new lands not quite so willingly, nor with so much power over those whose lives and lands they entered that they were able to become new dominators. In our era the Vietnamese and Sudanese have shown us how traumatic it can be to be forced from one's land by circumstances beyond one's control. Such immigrants are not expatriates and émigrés defined by promise and hope; they are exiles who live under the cloak of gloom and darkness. They became unwillingly separated from all that formerly gave them life and meaning.

Tamara Eskenazi notes: "The biblical account depicts exile as the state of a people who have just lost everything. The Babylonian exile meant to the Judeans . . . that the ground from under their feet was taken away, both literally and metaphorically."[21] National depression is the consequence of a people forced into exile. If a person experiences serious loss — home, job, loved ones — depression is almost impossible to avoid. This depression is compounded when it is unrecognized, dismissed, or denied. And what of the depression of a whole people forced to flee? The very group that would ordinarily offer meaning to such an individual is now itself devoid of meaning. The result can only be an anger turned inward. If experienced long enough, such collective depression can easily result in national anomie.

Many similarities to the trauma of the exile can be found in our church since the birth control ruling, the insistence that women not be ordained, and the pedophilia scandals that never addressed the underlying abuse of power. I also can find parallels close to home when some of us religious struggle with Rome over our efforts to declericalize our congregations. However, too often, rather than Edward Said's sense of grief that comes with exile as being "a condition of terminal loss,"[22] I find a kind of unrecognized understanding that such diminishment in confidence and numbers actually might be the only way God can purify an institution that will not be converted. As long as denials define our dilemmas and differences, especially in face of the destruction of dreams once dreamt, darkness and depression will determine our lives. This realization has made me ask where and to what degree we in the mainline religious congregations may be in denial about our gradual decline into increasing insignificance.

Consider our demographics. The majority of us who remain in religious life represent a generation that has been wandering around almost forty years since the council, but what about the next generation? Could it be that we have become the dry bones and they are the instruments of the spirit that might bring us to life (see Ezek. 37)? Could it be that the very concerns that triggered so many of our changes have no relevance for the Boomers and Generation X? They find irrelevant our debates about who is to be ordained, what gender is needed for marriages, and whether or not we use inclusive language. As we ensure our individualism and keep insisting on defining our "prophecy" in relation to these issues, could we just be the new *conservators* of a vision of church that doesn't speak to them in their search? Could this be the Spirit's invitation for us to probe more deeply into who we are and what will ground us? In the effort to challenge some of the rules and regulations of empire and *ekklēsía,* could we ourselves have ignored some of the weightier issues?

In the Exile, prophets like Ezekiel continually reminded the people that Jerusalem's fall had nothing to do with the triumph of foreign gods over theirs. Rather it was God's way of forcing the Israelites into purification, to getting back to authentically God-centered lives. Quite possibly our present disenchantment with where "we're at" and how we have diminished may be a gift of the Spirit trying to purify us as well. For exiles purification begins with grief over what has been lost; it continues with fear that few can even understand the source of this grief. Psalm 137 reminds us that the only place for exiles is to sit by the rivers of Babylon remembering a Jerusalem that is no more. This remembrance elicits grief for what has been lost and mourning for what may never be. As we sit and weep, the heavenly city still eludes us. However, in this grieving we are invited to become grounded in a deeper place. It beckons us not to look back but forward, to the promises held by the future rather than the shattered hopes of the past. Only in what might be, not what was, can we find another home. That "home" can be found in new ways of relating.

As a Franciscan experiencing exile, I find such hope in recalling Francis's recommendation of our need always to "remain in the abiding presence" of God in the face of such disturbances and upheavals. In his commentary on Francis's recommendation, Thomas of Celano also tells us that the only way such "Babylonian stuff" will be kept from increasing in our hearts will come when "it be at length driven out by tears." If this does not happen, the Babylonian stuff will "generate an abiding rust in the heart"[23] rather than an environment in which we will be grounded in the sense of God's abiding presence.

Tears, then, can be the way to purifying ourselves in the context of living within institutions that deny their need to be purified with their own tears of repentance. Such tears will represent the kind of grief that comes only when one can be assured that all attempts at preaching truth to power have been made, aware that this grief comes only when the poverty of powerlessness in the face of control gives way to the cry of care that echoes the compassion of God that knows no limits.

Being Carried into Captivity Leads to Contrition for the Circumstances That Caused It

In chapter 12 Ezekiel portrays Israel's Exile as a kind of "captivity" (12:11). Often I've used this image to refer to our situation as cultural and clerical captives under the domination of the imperial consciousness and the ideology of creeping infallibilism. Captives are those forced unwillingly to come under the power of outside and alien forces.

Especially when I was younger, I never thought of myself as being held in "captivity" by anyone; indeed I thought I was in control of my own destiny. I even told myself I was free and independent. But then I entered the order and came under the ideological control of those who said that whatever they told me was God's will. And I believed the lie. Once consciously freed of such clerical captivity, I felt as a young priest that I knew all the basic answers. I became what I had rejected. Nobody could challenge me; I couldn't be wrong. Not only was I right; I had to be right. But somewhere on my journey, people who loved me challenged me. Gradually I came to realize I'd become captive to my own individualistic ideology. I could find no truth anywhere but within myself. I had become clericalized.

Today my own ideological history enables my antennae to be attentive to ideology's mode of operating all around me. I hear it in voices of the talk show hosts on radio and television. It locates itself in the political discourse that seems intent on defining who's "in" and who's "out," who is a friend who enables and who is a foe who is evil. I find its slogans bandied about in conversations on patriotism regarding our political economy. Politicians offer selective use of facts, and we accept them as fiats. Even though headlines tell story after story of one corporate executive after another and this analyst and that accountant misleading the common folk, the citizenry still belie their cultural captivity to corporate capitalism by continued investments in high-flying stocks promising instant rewards. Meanwhile Ezekiel's words fall on deaf ears. Proclaiming that nothing shall remain, he noted what this "nothing" would be: "Not their abundance, not their wealth; no pre-eminence among them. The time has come, the day draws near; let not the buyer rejoice, nor the seller mourn, for wrath is upon their multitude" (Ezek. 7:11–12).

When it comes to many parts of the institutional church, I find the effort to hold us captive expressed in the attitude of certitude that the male, celibate, clerical model of church is what God wills. We watch our parishes close, merge, and melt down as the Eucharist is sacrificed on the altar of male celibacy. Such untrinitarian (and, therefore, ungodly and idolatrous) thinking makes words from Ezekiel sound very apropos: "You also took your beautiful jewels of my gold and my silver that I had given you, and made for yourself male images" (Ezek. 16:17). The male image of God dominates Catholicism; sooner or later such an image will be abandoned by those who have discovered the truth. Until then we will suffer from a kind of "cultural captivity to clericalism" that makes us a people of dry bones, even as we proclaim ourselves to be quite alive.

Karl Marx said two of the main roles for ideology are to serve a group's self-interests and to make its adherents incapable of self-criticism. Whether of a political, economic, or religious brand, ideology immunizes its adherents from self-critique. Without self-critique, there can be no conversion. Without conversion, inspiration becomes insipid. When such immunization from critique becomes the pattern among a people, we are unlikely to be healed.

At this point, lest I be called unpatriotic to the president or disloyal to the pope, I want to be clear I love my country and believe in the magisterium — in their best meanings, free of simple equations with their trappings and the unquestioned power that accompanies them. As a citizen of this land, I have found a good distinction in the bumper sticker that declares: "I love my country but disagree with its leaders." As a Franciscan this means that any obedience I pledge to superiors can never be limited only to the pope, nor the bishops nor the people alone. The magisterium is given to *the church,* and the statements of our leaders must flow from and into the best sense of what the faithful believe. As the saying goes, "You can't have one without the other."

One time, as I was preparing comments about the aberrations regarding "church" when we limit its meaning to what I call "the Church of Matthew 16" to the exclusion of "the Church of Matthew 18," I happened to talk with a friend about what I'd be saying. Hearing my comments she protested: "Mike, the magisterium is an anchor. We need that." I agreed. At the same time, however, as we teased out the anchor image, it became clear that all worthwhile anchors themselves must be grounded in something outside themselves. In our church, especially among those hierarchs who claim sole authority, this ground must be that triune God who has been revealed in Jesus Christ. It is the Spirit of that Jesus who serves both the apostolic charism and the prophetic charism. Otherwise, if the anchor has too much weight (or is given too much weight) and has no grounding itself, it can destroy the whole boat and drown all who did not know how to get out and swim for shore. I believe we are witnesses to the consequences of such false thinking as we see more and more honest and thinking people "abandoning ship."

I got a glimpse of a process that might help free us from our various forms of captivity when I met periodically in 1994 with some members of Call to Action, one of the various reform groups within the U.S. Catholic Church. Originally we convened to discuss what we might do in response to that year's Republican sweep of the U.S. Congress. Ostensibly we gathered to develop political strategy that might serve as a challenge to what had occurred. However, the more we shared, the deeper we found ourselves moving in another direction — into a probe of issues about our own spirituality. As our trust developed, we sheepishly had to admit that many of us had overly identified with the Democratic Party to the point that we found ourselves silent as the religious right was used by Republicans to further its agenda. Not wanting to be manipulated in our faith, we found that we had become compromised in our confession, confused and even quiet about its consequences. For some of us our politics had little soul; others even began wondering aloud whether, in our efforts at social change, we had become spiritually bankrupt. As the trust grew even deeper, we began asking ourselves who Jesus was for us and what it might mean for him to be the Christ in today's culture. We questioned what would happen if we consciously saw ourselves as his followers in this generation. We began sharing what our justice agenda might entail if it really were infused with faith. In the process of sharing we realized our trust in each other had enabled us to be free of our various kinds of captivity. We were beginning to discover a truth that was setting us free. As we parted company, we knew that our conversation had enabled us to become a community of trust in the midst of our exile. Our grounding had come in the coming-together and the hope it provided.

Of all the prophets, only Ezekiel declared that infidelity to God had been Israel's sin from the beginning (see chapters 20 and 23 particularly). Indeed, he said that Israel had *never been obedient* to the Lord.[24] What might this mean to us? Could such a condemnatory stance have resonance today?

Politically, has the United States, which was formed to be a nation acknowledging that all *men* are created equal, ever really been totally committed to equality under the law for its citizens and the citizens of the world? Since this has never been realized, why should we wonder why so many are silent as one of its presidents works to free the country of the jurisdiction of the International Criminal Court? Or economically, despite political promises about equal pay for equal work, why is it that women and minorities still do not get paid the same as white males?[25] Why, with its imperial power buttressed by military might, do the United States and its citizens continue to think of themselves in ways shared by none others in the world? Are we, the 5 percent, the only correct ones?

Next, as I consider my alien status as a Catholic, I wonder if we or our leaders in the Roman Church have ever submitted ourselves to fulfill what it means to have the Spirit of the Risen Christ direct our lives in a way that will bring about the reign of God. The realization that we have all failed should invite us to conversion, especially through words and deeds of repentance. However, this repentance cannot be absolved by a gesture of regret like saying "I'm sorry." Neither is it sufficient for a pope to apologize for the sins of "certain children of the church." Continuing the "confessional" image, for authentic absolution to occur there must be a resolve to "sin no more." More than reinstating meatless Fridays or mandating days of official mourning, we must transform those petty and self-serving individual and institutional ideologies into structures that evoke the majesty and mystery of the inclusive trinitarian God.

We often quote Galatians: "There is no longer Jew or Greek, there is no longer slave or free, there is no longer male and female; for all of you are one in Christ Jesus" (Gal. 3:28). Yet we fail to implement its vision in our very institution, especially in regard to women. Even though the First Ecumenical Council at Jerusalem institutionalized Paul's insight regarding Jews and Gentiles, our church still struggles over a document apologizing to the Jews for its anti-Semitism. While it took eighteen hundred years to accept the political and economic implications of being followers of a Christ in whom there is "no longer slave or free," yet only now are some of us who are members of religious congregations that held slaves beginning to address the sin this entailed.

Despite the residue, I think, as an institution, we have made substantial changes in two of the three areas that Galatians indicates the Spirit must be allowed to work in the church if it is to be free of the works of the flesh. Being no longer divided between Jew and Gentile, slave or free, makes it all the more mandatory that we address the third area of inequality: that between women and men. This invites us to ask: What but cultural captivity is keeping us from addressing the issue of sexism in the church?

The Way of Vengeance Based on Exclusion Gives Way to Wisdom Based in Compassion

Edward Said offered the insight that exiles tend to reflect the either/or approach to life when they "look at non-exiles with resentment. *They* belong in their surroundings, you feel, whereas an exile is always out of place."[26] While this may be true of many contemporary exiles, during Israel and Judah's sojourn in Babylon, providentially, another attitude developed once the people realized that God's identity could no longer be equated with the institutions of territory and temple. The once dominating and patriarchal images of God became more balanced by a more inclusive understanding of God that revealed feminine characteristics.[27] Feminist critics of the Israelite prophetic tradition have noted the ways it suppressed goddess worship (see Jer. 44:15–19) and interpreted Israel not only as a dependent virgin and adulterous wife but also as an unfaithful harlot. It must be remembered, however, that this kind of negative imaging was balanced by passages in Hosea that speak of God as a bear robbed of her cubs (Hos. 13:8); by Second Isaiah, who speaks of God in terms of a woman in labor (Isa. 42:14) by Third Isaiah, whose God comforts her children like a woman (Isa. 66:13); and by Jeremiah, who can talk of a God who takes up the cry of Rachel weeping for her children (Jer. 31:15–20).

While the people of the Exile never embraced an image of God as female to balance their masculine notion of God, the upheaval involved in the Exile did challenge the people to begin to change their understanding of God as vengeful to God as a force full of mercy. This experience evoked in Israel's hopes a particular form of God's mercy, which began to be described in the more inclusive and feminine image of compassion (*ruhamah*). Indeed for Dianne Bergant, compassion "informs all divine activity" and, as such, is "a controlling metaphor in the Bible."[28]

One of the Hebrew words that has been translated as "compassion" is *rahamim*, a word derived from the root *rehem*, or "womb." Jeremiah gave voice to God's word when he prophesied: "Therefore my womb trembles for him [Israel]; I will truly show motherly compassion" (Jer. 31:20). Here God changes "his" self-designation as male with Israel as the female; God is feminine with a womb that trembles for "him," i.e., Israel. An examination of these words (*rahamim* and *rehem*) illuminates, Dianne Bergant says, "the meaning of one of the most prominent characterizations of God present in the Bible."[29] With no home in their given land or religion, God's people needed to find their home in another womb. They needed to return to the principle of their life in order to abide in God's loving presence. There they could be called to emerge as recipients and mediators of God's compassion in a troubled world.

Although we hear political and economic image after image related to "compassionate conservatism" and the like, it is not always easy to find examples of people whose "hearts are moved with compassion" as Jesus' heart was (see Matt. 9:36; 14:14; 15:32; 20:34; Mark 1:41; 6:34; 8:2; Luke 7:13; see Matt. 18:27; Luke 10:33; 15:20). I've found, though, an honest exemplification of true compassion in a literary figure, namely, Shug, in

Alice Walker's *The Color Purple*. In a conversation between Shug and Celie, two Southern black women, the discussion turns to their ways of imaging God. Shug tells Celie that she thought "God was white, and a man," and so she "lost interest." Shug then says: "God ain't a he or a she, but a It." Celie continues:

> But what do it look like? I ast.
>
> Don't look like nothing, she say. It ain't a picture show. It ain't something you can look at apart from anything else, including yourself. . . .
>
> She say, My first step from [thinking about God as] the old white man was trees. Then air. Then birds. Then other people. But one day when I was sitting quiet and feeling like a motherless child, which I was, it come to me: that feeling of being part of everything, not separate at all. I knew that if I cut a tree, my arm would bleed. And I laughed and I cried and I run all around the house. I knew just what it was. In fact, when it happens you can't miss it.[30]

Shug received her insight in a way that can be understood as universal compassion. In this experience, this Southern black woman, a descendent of slaves, shows she has learned the wisdom of her ancestors in their exile. The exile, be it imposed, as it was for her ancestors, or realized, as it was for Shug, teaches us that the way of God is the way of compassion and wisdom. In boundary-less Babylon, I believe, our only place of rest can be the womb of compassionate wisdom. What a dream this can be for us who have tired of political correctness and conventional wisdom. What a hope it can instill in us who still yearn for our dried bones to be inspirited with some newly graced energy that moves beyond ministering only at the individual and interpersonal levels to include the infrastructural and environmental levels as well.

Levels of Our World	Economy Level	Task of Formation	Goal of Spirituality
Individual	*Oikía*	Therapeutic	Healing
Interpersonal	*Oikonomía*	Communitarian	Reconciliation
Infrastructural	*Oikoumēne*	Prophetic	Justice
Environmental	*Oikología*	Unitive	Compassion

When I try to chart how this might be done at the four levels that we have explained, I find the need for formation programs and spirituality itself to integrate all four levels rather than being defined by any one in isolation from the others. Since God is at the heart of all creation, we must find ourselves at every level of creation as well, not just the first and second levels to the exclusion of the third or the third without addressing issues related to the first two. By being present at the first three levels we will be more ready to do the integrative work that grounds us in the fourth level, the unitive way of compassion.

If people are not "at home" (*oikía*) with themselves at the individual level, formation must stress a therapeutic approach that they may be healed in order to begin growing in their spirituality. If groups are unable to relate or share together (*oikonomía*), the task of formation must enable them to be reconciled. However, when reconciliation cannot be effected because of inequality, formation for the prophetic life demands that justice be proclaimed to alleviate the wrong. This necessitates a challenge to the underlying ideology that sustains the "isms" in so many of the institutions that perpetuate that injustice that characterizes our *oikoumēne*. Finally, when we work to integrate all three levels of the world and its households in ways that ensure healing, reconciliation, and justice, we will have laid the groundwork for a way of life and a deep *oikología* in our exile that enables us to be at one with all that exists in creation. We will have discovered the wisdom that speaks cosmic compassion. We will have entered more fully into the reign of God that we have proclaimed.

Babylon's Seductive Culture Must Be Countered by the Creation of Communities of Resistance

Ezekiel did not limit his oracles to his own political, economic, and religious institution (Ezek. 4–24); his attacks were directed against the surrounding nations as well (Ezek. 25–32). As we consider our efforts at social justice in the wider political and economic spheres, he might teach us a few tactics. One of Ezekiel's clever strategies was not to attack Babylon directly. Instead he prophesied against the surrounding nations for activities practiced in and among his own people. One of these nations was Tyre, the small Hong Kong-like territory that, like its contemporary counterpart, wielded huge economic power (Ezek. 26:1–28:24).

As we struggle against the seductive spells of our own Babylons, it's not hard to find parallels. For instance, despite significant statements from the pope on the "savagery" of our capitalist brand of political economy,[31] too often we, the church, represent the managerial and business class and subscribe uncritically to its interests. In the process, we have distanced ourselves from the working class here and abroad. For too many of us, our brand of capitalism, in effect, has become our religion; not only have we become indoctrinated into its mores, we have become its altar servers.[32] Deep down, none of us want it to fail, especially in times when it seems to be foundering; after all, this would adversely affect our portfolios.

As we continue to struggle, those of us who have not been totally acculturated by the dominant culture of empire and *ekklēsía* somehow intuit that the only way we will find meaning in our individual exile will be with like-minded people in some alternative grouping.

Edward Said writes that the "pathos of exile is in the loss of contact with the solidity and the satisfaction of earth: homecoming is out of the question."[33] In this same spirit, Ezekiel prophesied to the people to create an alternative community to keep from being totally without bearings. In chapter 9 Yahweh told Ezekiel in a vision: "Go through the city, through Jerusalem, and put a mark on the foreheads of those who sigh and groan over all the abominations that are committed in it" (9:4). In Ezekiel those who accepted the need for change were to be marked with a sign to be inscribed on their foreheads.

> *Despite significant statements from the pope on the "savagery" of our capitalist brand of political economy, too often we, the church, represent the managerial and business class and subscribe uncritically to its interests.*

If Ezekiel envisioned in a remnant an alternative to a Jerusalem in desolation and Francis discerned that an alternative community would be his response to a church falling into ruins, it seems we're headed in the right direction if we do the same in our exile. However, this alternative community cannot be perceived just as a subset of the wider whole; the wider whole must be re-established through these communities. It must not be a church with communities but a church of communities. Small communities cannot be regarded as a practical way we express ourselves as church; they must be the preferred way.

Recalling Max Weber's model of charism and prophecy, I believe we will find energy in our exile only when the dead bones represented in the institutionalization of the charisms of our founders will come alive in the nurturing and support found in the creation of alternative communities that give voice to the prophetic character of our life that has been lost. For too long we have tried to make sure "all are on board"; in the process we have found ourselves on a sinking ship. This demands that we find the Spirit bringing dry bones to life in the creation of alternative communities that bring a new kind of prophetic criticism and energy to their gatherings.

The Indifference Generated in Face of Long-Standing Structures of Control Gives Way to a New Vision of Hope

One of the most memorable parts of Ezekiel involves God's pledge that Israel would be given God's own spirit (Ezek. 37:14). However, the whole context for Israel's sharing in the very spirit of God takes place in the midst of Ezekiel's description of Israel as being a heap of dry bones. If we have experienced ambiguity, anomie or, worse still, an asphyxiation of our spirits as we consider our present milieu, perhaps the image of the dry bones coming to life with a new spirit might give us new energy to continue walking with like-minded companions.

Like many people in concentration camps, exiles without a sense of purpose, without meaning, will never experience hope. But for exiles anchored in God's presence, power, and promises, hope provides energy for a transformed life charged with meaning. Hope tells us that, even in Babylon, with God's presence in our midst, no higher authority can claim our hearts and no other god can control our allegiance. As Walter Brueggemann puts it: "Babylon cannot stop the energizing of God."[34]

However, reading this, we should not become naively optimistic. As we begin to find our energy from an exilic spirituality, like Ezekiel, we need to watchful (see Ezek. 3:16–21; 33:1–4) lest our hope begins to be linked

with a certain kind of restoration of the old ways. Beneath exile's assumptions there often can lurk a false expectation. Ezekiel, like the other exilic
prophets, always held out the hope of some kind of political restoration
for Israel. And, indeed, for Israel, it did come to pass. However, I don't
think such will occur for us — at least not in our lifetime. I know many
Catholics envision a kind of "restoration" of the institutional church to
its former patriarchal and triumphalistic ways. Yet, given the way science
and philosophy have evolved, I think we fool ourselves if we imagine
ourselves heading toward some kind of Promised Land or Restoration in
the sense of having a politically or even culturally powerful church again.
We must find hope for any "restoration" grounded in places removed from
former locales. This will never again be identified with institutionalized religion as much as with biblical spirituality, especially the kind of prophetic
spirituality whose elements I've tried to outline here.

As I conclude this chapter, I offer a summary of the prophetic spirituality I've tried to outline for us in the here and now that I've called
"Exile." Such a spirituality for exiles involves three elements: an inner,
an outer, and a communal dimension. It comprises (1) an experience of
God that (2) is expressed in concrete ways (3) in the context of some
kind of community. I've suggested that a spirituality for exiles invites us to
continually be open to God's immanent presence in our midst and to find
ways to worship God's transcendence in rituals that do not box God in
with human categories. It challenges us to create boundaries characterized
by compassion — toward creation and the "crowd" — in ways modeled on
Jesus' reinterpretation of the traditional holiness codes. Its actualization
demands that, as we find ourselves "unwanted" or not "at home" within
the religious and cultural institutions that previously nurtured us, we keep
coming together seeking the wisdom that arises in us from the Spirit and
from being part of a community of hope.

Hope equips us in our exile to wait in confident expectation for what
lies ahead. Hope roots us in a reality that is not yet realized. Hope ignites
our imagination in a release of the Spirit's energy within and among us.
Hope invites us to recognize that "everywhere" can be home and that
all our "whenevers" can be *kairós* moments of grace. Hope, Brueggemann
reminds us, is: "the 'wind of God' which creates a new future. That wind
is beyond resistance from the empire or anyone else."[35]

In novitiate, one of my favorite poems was Charles Péguy's "Hope," and one of its verses is, to my mind, the perfect summation of my preceding reflections: "Faith is she who remains steadfast during centuries and centuries. Charity is she who gives herself during centuries and centuries. But my little hope is she who gets up every morning."[36]

Five

The Prophetic Witness of Non-Assent and Non-Submission

The Challenge of Being Prophetic in the Midst of Imperial Injustice

There are many benefits to living in an empire, and its acolytes, especially those religious who receive grants from various corporate entities, will have no difficulty in articulating what these are. However, when one has been overwhelmed with the experience of God as the ground of all reality, those testimonies on behalf of empire invariably are exposed as deficient.

In chapter 2, I noted that, as far back as 1971, when the bishops of the Catholic Church met in Synod, they declared:

> Even though it is not for us to elaborate a very profound analysis of the situation of the world, we have nevertheless been able to perceive the serious injustices which are building around the world of men a network of domination, oppression and abuses which stifle freedom and which keep the greater part of humanity from sharing in the building up and enjoyment of a more just and more fraternal world.[1]

When injustice defines the ways of the empire, civil dissent and civil disobedience are mandated for people of moral integrity.

The necessity of civil disobedience for the good of the nation has been a part of the very framework of the United States since its beginning. Indeed, Thomas Jefferson believed that, in the course of human events, it would occur that, given the rise of unjust systems, people would be bound to rise up when those governments they created no longer served their interests as the governed. An actual notion of civil disobedience as such first was articulated by Henry David Thoreau in his classic 1849 essay, "Civil Disobedience."[2] Opposed to the institutionalization of slavery as well as to what he considered to be the U.S. imperialistic war against Mexico, Thoreau refused to pay war taxes. Forgotten for a little over a century, his writings were dusted off during the Vietnam War. At that time he became a critical source to justify the withholding of taxes by those who considered that war to be unjust.

In the same year that the bishops of the Catholic Church met to discuss "Justice in the World" (1971), John Rawls published his now-classic *A Theory of Justice*. He defines civil disobedience "as a public, nonviolent, conscientious yet political act contrary to law usually done with the aim of bringing about a change in the law or policies of the government."[3] Since civil disobedience is not difficult to justify in the context of a corrupt regime that refuses to address the needs or follow the will of the majority, Rawls concerned himself rather with justifying civil disobedience within a nation that considers itself "just" but actually is not. When such social self-delusion defines the situation, the disobedient minority will find themselves outside the "mainstream," alienated from the majority. Rawls outlines principles justifying conscientious objection as well as civil non-cooperation for such situations. He offers justifications for dissent and disobedience in cases where the majority affirms and submits to (if not embraces) the government's fiats.

A classic case where Catholics have been invited to object conscientiously as well as to disobey can be found in the hierarchy's teachings related to noncooperation with the 1973 decision of the U.S. Supreme Court that gave women the right to terminate their pregnancies. The result was that, in the year 2000 (the latest year for which figures are available), there were 21.3 abortions for every 1,000 women ages fifteen to forty-four. Documenting the fact that a majority consider abortion justified, a *USA Today*/CNN Gallup Poll showed in 2003 that only 38 percent of the adults responding supported a constitutional amendment to ban abortion in all circumstances, except when necessary to save the life of the mother.[4]

What is one to do when one's conscience says this is wrong in a nation that justifies it and legalizes it in its juridical system?

In its "Declaration on Procured Abortion," the Congregation for the Doctrine of the Faith argued, from a rights perspective, that the right to life takes precedence over all other rights. When the U.S. Supreme

Court in *Roe v. Wade* allowed abortion, it argued in favor of a woman's secondary right (to privacy) over a primary right (to life). Though citizens of the nation, the Catholic bishops would not endorse the rationale. They prophetically declared: "We reject this decision of the Court because, as John XXIII says, 'if any government does not acknowledge the rights of man or violates them...its orders completely lack juridical force.'"[5] Echoing the U.S. bishops the Vatican itself stated: "a Christian can never conform to a law which is in itself immoral."[6]

How this nonconformity takes place will be resolved in each person's conscience. For me it has been to help investors steer away from stocks in companies that manufacture birth control pills that result in abortions. It also led me in 1976, in my former capacity as chair of the Milwaukee Priests' Senate Justice and Peace Committee, to support the right of conscience exercised by fellow priests and others who withhold that percentage of monies from their taxes that is used for funding abortions. More recently, I urged the leaders of the mainline women's and men's religious orders in the U.S.A. (LCWR and CMSM) to be more visible in opposing abortion. At their joint Assembly in Fort Worth in August 2004, I said:

> When we consider the witness that we make with government through Network and corporations through our shareholder actions, I think we are being prophetic. But I also believe our counterparts in the Council of Major Superiors of Women Religious in the U.S.A., who were introduced yesterday, also believe they are being "prophetic" as well insofar as they are challenging politicians on the left by their witness and picketing at clinics providing abortions in their effort to support life. I also think that many of them have found a way of living simply and austerely and being in solidarity with the poor that is a source of secret admiration and wonder on our part. So I think they can rightfully, at least in these areas, see themselves as prophetic (even though I also see them as "house" or "royal" prophets insofar as they fully embrace whatever is said by the clerics in our church on ecclesiastical issues with no independent stance of their own).
>
> In this sense, I do wish, however, that we'd find a way of delinking ourselves, at least de facto, by also challenging our politicians to be equally concerned about other right-to-life issues than those

which have characterized our efforts, such as human rights, especially abortion. In this way we could never be accused of being one sided and, thus, open to being used. I think we also would be more inclusive and faithful to the whole "seamless garment" that is core to an integral Catholic approach to social justice. My Capuchin brother Dan continually reminds me of our need to be "both/and" people rather than "either/or." If we would find a way of doing this linking I think we would be more truly prophetic and consistent in our public witness.[7]

Every person and, especially, all religious, must determine not whether, but how (and how far), they will speak their truth to power and accept the consequences this might entail. In this they can receive support in the words of the Congregation for the Doctrine of the Faith:

> Following one's conscience in obedience to the law of God is not always the easy way. One must not fail to recognize the weight of the sacrifices and the burdens which it can impose. Heroism is sometimes called for in order to remain faithful to the requirements of the Divine law. Therefore we must emphasize that the path of true progress of the human person passes through this constant fidelity to a conscience maintained in uprightness and truth; and we must exhort all those who are able to do so to lighten the burdens still crushing so many men and women, families and children, who are placed in situations to which in human terms there is not solution.[8]

Such arguments might be kept in mind as we now turn to the demands of prophecy in the face of our increasingly clericalized church.

The Challenge of Being Prophetic in a Clerical Church: A Case Study

In its August 2, 2002, edition the *National Catholic Reporter* published in its "Briefs" an incident in which I was involved and which was treated briefly in this book's introduction: the election of one of our nonordained brothers to be our minister provincial or, canonically, our highest superior at the provincial level. It read:

In early June, the Vatican rejected a religious brother chosen as provincial minister of the Detroit-based St. Joseph Province of the Order of Friars Minor Capuchin.

Capuchin Franciscan Br. Robert Smith, president of Messmer High School in Milwaukee, was elected by provincial members to lead the province for three years. His election was confirmed by the Capuchins' Rome-based general minister, Fr. John Corriveau, but was rejected by the Vatican's Congregation for Institutes of Consecrated Life and Societies of Apostolic Life.[9]

Our elections in June 2002 took place in the context of our solemn realization that we are a group of Franciscans in the Roman Church who believe the Holy Spirit must be the inspiration and ultimate authority in our decision-making. In this conviction we began our election process with solemn prayers asking the Holy Spirit to guide our vote. The election had been proceeded by extended public and private conversations regarding the dilemma we faced. On the one hand, we were committed to the following of our Rule approved by Rome. Its wording makes it clear that all offices are open to all perpetually professed friars. On the other hand, we are part of the Rome of today, and today the Roman Curia has made it clear that the highest offices in groups like ours are to be reserved to clerical members only. Given the conflict between a Rome "of the past," which approved our Rule — which enabled nonclerics to be the head of the order — and a Rome "of the present," which is intent on extending the male clerical model of the church wherever it can, we relied on the Holy Spirit who is the same yesterday, today, and forever. We turned our deliberations over to this Spirit to guide our individual and corporate conscience about our future leadership.

In such a conflict between the apostolic function and the charismatic function, it was inevitable that frustration would characterize our deliberations, especially since we knew well the recent history of the Curia's unwillingness to change its position on the matter — not because of theological arguments presented nor because of the truth of the matter itself — but simply because of the clerical tradition.

Fully conscious of the dilemma we faced, we elected Robert Smith on the first ballot by a solid plurality of the 150-plus eligible voting members.

He would have received even more votes, but many of those voting for another friar indicated they did so not wanting to be humiliated by Rome as a province or to have Bob hurt by an anticipated negative decision, despite the fact that many believed him to be the right person for this ministry. We also had been warned by the minister general of the order, our highest authority, that, should we try to finesse Rome by giving him the title "president" (along with our obedience) while giving the canonical title "provincial" to a cleric (who would serve as a figurehead), Rome might suppress the order itself. Despite such premonitions and warnings, we elected Bob Smith.

As the *National Catholic Reporter* article noted, "the Capuchins expected the Vatican to reject Smith's election," and so another friar was then chosen by us in case Rome rejected our choice. We had to resort to this vote, not because we necessarily believed we were being led by the Spirit to do so, but for purely practical reasons: we did not want to return to elect another friar later if there was such a real chance our Spirit-led choice would be rejected by Rome.

This event was not the first time our belief in the Holy Spirit's guidance over our deliberations would be countered by the Vatican. In 1987, a nonordained brother, David Schwab, was elected vicar provincial (i.e., a major superior) by us only to be rejected by the Congregation for Institutes of Consecrated Life and Societies of Apostolic Life (CICLSAL). That time we seemed to have exhibited a little more prophetic "imagination" than fifteen years later. We named him "assistant provincial" and gave him our authority to function effectively as the vicar provincial. This time we were warned not to do something similar, lest we risk the dissolution of the province and possibly the suppression of the order itself. Consequently the freedom of the Spirit was undermined by the fear of reprisals — hardly a sign of the fruits of the Spirit but a clear manifestation, to me, of the works of the flesh. Indeed, if Paul in Galatians is correct about the signs indicating the fruits of the Spirit (esp. Gal. 5:20), it seemed such threats indicated the whole process ultimately was being led by the flesh over the Spirit (esp. Gal. 5:20).

Our experience as a province and our treatment by Rome have not been dissimilar to the experience of several other provinces in the order or other groups similar to ours. In my opinion the whole context of elections undertaken by invoking the Holy Spirit made a mockery of a key element in the efforts at renewal we and so many others had made since the Second Vatican Council. Following the mandate of the Council and subsequent Vatican statements on the appropriate renewal of religious life, we Capuchin Franciscans had revisited the charism of our founders, Francis and Clare. We determined we had been founded as a community of equals. However, as in many religious movements, as noted in the model of Weber explained in the first chapter, over history we too had become clericalized. Attempting to recapture the original vision, we declared in our constitutions that all offices in the order would be open to all perpetually professed brothers.

When our leaders submitted the final work of the friars, the Vatican refused to accept this part of our Constitutions; it demanded instead that the order define itself as "clerical." After years of meetings between our representatives and Vatican officials, the curial congregation overseeing religious life insisted that we Capuchins put into our Constitutions a statement that would acknowledge our identity as clerical. Effectively such a provision would limit the highest offices only to clerics. Having exhausted any more efforts to reach an understanding with the Curia, the General Council (called "The Definitory") appealed to the pope.

After some time, word was received that, after due consideration of the Capuchin request, it was now the decision of the Holy See that the order declare in its Constitutions that it was to be a clerical order.

When the decree was received, it happened that a Polish member of the General Definitory knew a Polish secretary of Pope John Paul II. He inquired of his countryman about the rationale as to why the pope would reject the Capuchins' request. The Polish secretary responded with another question: "What request?" At that the Capuchin leaders realized that curial officials had used the term "Holy See" as a cover to make our leaders think that it was the pope's decision to clericalize the order. Meanwhile these curial officials had arrogated to themselves so much power that they had not even submitted the request to the pope; indeed, they apparently felt their decisions could be defined as those of the pope himself.

At that point I decided I needed to speak my "truth to power." My letter to the cardinal in charge read in part:

Most Reverend and Dear Cardinal Martinez Somalo:

...The entire question about Robert Smith must be grounded in the non-negotiable acceptance of the equality of all our men in solemn vows. The fact that ministers in our Order might not be priests was, in fact, inscribed in the Rule of 1223 which was *approved by Rome*. Speaking of the "brothers who sin" it said: "If any of the brothers...sin mortally in regard to those sins about which it may have been decreed among the brothers to have recourse *only to the ministers provincial* such brothers must have recourse to them as soon as possible, without delay. *If these ministers are priests,* they shall impose a penance upon them with mercy; *but if they are not priests,* they shall have it imposed by other priests of the Order as it seems best to them according to God."

Francis of Assisi simply accepted as a given that some ministers of the Order would be ordained and others would not; thus the above paragraph is not even part of the section on authority in the Order! The ministry of authority in our Order has nothing to do with orders in the Church.

For CICLSAL to insist on something contrary to the intent of Francis and the early practice of the Order and our Reform would be a violation of the spirit and intent of Vatican II. It would also be further evidence that, to preserve the traditional, clerical model of the Roman Church, CICLSAL seems willing to impose that model even among those congregations wherein it never was intended originally. This further erodes the credibility of the pope and the Curia. It also creates further embarrassment for those of us who are trying to be faithful as loyal Roman Catholics in the face of the abuse of power exercised by many church leaders. As we in the U.S. experience the abuse of power by some of our own bishops we who are in the Midwest Province of the Capuchin Franciscans now find further evidence, at the highest levels of the institutional church, of one more abuse of power in the way our discernment has been rejected by the Curia for almost fifteen years....

Sincerely yours,

s./ *(Rev.) Michael H. Crosby, O.F.M.Cap.*

While the above may be a specific case faced by my own congregation the incident is not isolated. It also reveals deeper issues that demand honest discussion. Incidentally, my letter was never acknowledged.

The Role of Non-Assent in the Roman Church

Given that the tradition has so often muffled the voice of the prophet if not muzzled it completely, the task of unmasking the clerical consciousness that has numbed the imagination of almost all in the institutional church will be daunting. Abuses of hierarchical power that have been noted as widespread in the press (and lesser-known ones in reference to groups like us Capuchin Franciscans) undermine the legitimate and considered use of power by the papacy and its curial offices. What, then, is the proper role of non-assent as well as non-submission in the Roman Church? A nuance made by the theologian Lawrence S. Cunningham is critical:

> All would agree that there can be no discussion when it comes to the creedal articulations of the church or defined doctrines of faith.... [But] there are patently moments when it is possible or *even obligatory* for people to dissent from certain church practices. It is perfectly legitimate for someone to say that clerical celibacy ought to be abolished for the diocesan priesthood and not be a dissenter. It may even be demanded to say that this or that bishop ought to resign for abuses of power in office as has happened in fact quite recently.[10]

Cunningham's distinctions are all the more important when we recall the problem we face in the Roman Church when the charisms of apostolic authority and prophetic utterance are compromised in their original integrity. This occurs when the charismatic functioning once identified with apostolic authority claims control over all other charisms. It is legitimated when the notion of authority in the church itself is usurped by its clerical expression to the exclusion of the authority of the faithful. It is culturally reinforced when any challenge is interpreted as infidelity. How this pattern of thinking has evolved has been the subject of much debate, but one concrete consequence of the situation is that those who publicly disagree with various decrees (not dogmas) of the magisterium that reflect the "Church of Matthew 16" are in jeopardy, even though their position may reflect that of the "Church of Matthew 18."

One of the clearest examples of a religious congregation in public disagreement with an order from Rome came in 2001 with the Erie, Pennsylvania, Benedictines. Vatican officials told the religious superior of Sister Joan Chittister, O.S.B., to prohibit her from addressing the Worldwide Women's Ordination Conference in Dublin. Torn between Rome's understanding of obedience, which demanded that she submit to its ruling, and her own understanding of obedience as contained in the Benedictine Rule, Constitutions, and traditions, the prioress, Sr. Christine Vladimiroff, O.S.B., decided to take the problem to the Erie community. After much discussion in the community, a vote was taken. All but one of the 128 sisters involved supported her decision not to prohibit Joan from speaking. Their conclusion made it clear: Rome's understanding of obedience was not the Benedictine approach.

The result was a media frenzy, just one more incident in the ever-widening storm that was tearing apart any previous calm connected to the way power was being (ab)used by clerics in the church. Later, Sr. Christine offered reflections that serve as the basis of the following discussion on dissent and disobedience in the church: "Contrary to some headlines in newspapers, it was not an act of dissent, but an act of deep and abiding loyalty. It was not an act of defiance, but a gesture of profound love. It was not an act of disobedience, but an act of fidelity to the spirit speaking within."[11] Such insights stopped further action on the part of the Vatican in that case.

A little-developed teaching of the Second Vatican Council in its Dogmatic Constitution the Church, *Lumen Gentium,* states that "the holy People of God shares also in Christ's prophetic office." This means that "the body of the faithful as a whole, anointed as they are by the Holy One (cf. John 2:20, 27), cannot err in matters of belief." It is the church itself, "the People as a whole," that is gifted with infallibility; no entity within the whole can arrogate infallibility to itself without undermining the teaching of the church. The "People of God" include "the bishops to the last of the faithful."[12] One of the bishops who is part of the People of God is the bishop of Rome.

Poll after poll makes it evident that two key teachings of the clerical church have not been embraced by the faithful. These are found in the

Vatican teachings on birth control, especially *Casti Connubii* (1930) and *Humanae Vitae* (1968), and the ordination of women as found in *Inter Insigniores* (1976) and *Ordinatio Sacerdotalis* (1994). Acknowledging that the polls may be useful in determining the degree to which church teaching is accepted by the faithful, John E. Thiel goes further in showing that "reception" is deeper than polls:

> Although appeal may be made to social-scientific data in testing the reception of doctrine in the Church, one must rely finally on the sense of the faith itself in judging whether doctrine has been received by the faithful, who in turn evaluate the legitimacy of the judgment. In any case, defining the unerring faithful as those who receive all magisterial teaching in faith and practice wrongly equates the infallibility of the Church with obedience to the magisterium in any particular historical moment, and ignores both the dynamics of doctrinal development and the fact of dramatic development in the tradition.[13]

The fact that the degree of receptivity to *Casti Connubii* was probably much higher than that given *Humanae Vitae* thirty-eight years later, as well as the fact that the number of people believing women can be ordained was higher in 1994 with *Ordinatio Sacerdotalis* than in 1976 with *Inter Insigniores,* attest to the logic of Thiel's position. The pews are thinking.

One determinant of whether a doctrine in the Roman Church might be judged to be in the process of development (which, therefore, mitigates the degree of required adherence) deals with the character of the theological argumentation presented in the teaching. That a teaching is in the process of being developed can be determined by three criteria: circumstantial, logical, and rhetorical factors. Of these three related elements that mitigate adherence to institutional teaching, Thiel writes:

> First, argument is deemed necessary because the teaching addresses changing cultural circumstances in which a simple reiteration of traditional doctrine would not suffice. Argument serves as a way of mediating traditional meaning to novel issues, problems, or situations. Second, argument is deemed necessary because this mediated teaching requires a specific and conflicting application of the tradition's more basic beliefs, an application that represents a movement

to doctrine more derivative, though not necessarily less authoritative. Logic (here following its traditional rules!) serves the magisterium by demonstrating the reasonableness of the application, by showing how the teaching's conclusion derives its authority from a major premise (more basic beliefs) rightly modified by its minor (changing cultural circumstances). Third, argument is deemed necessary because unanimity in the Church is lacking for the doctrine in question. Argument thus has the rhetorical goal of persuasion.[14]

In dealing with non-assent and even dissent from "official" church teachings, legitimate disagreement must address the arguments, it is true. However, this qualification is compounded when the "official" church teachers effectively establish themselves unilaterally as the sole interpreter of the Scriptures and tradition with no involvement of other than "establishment theologians," much less the faithful. When this approach is combined with Rome's undialogical stance, those thinking otherwise have no avenue open but non-assent when such teaching goes against their conscience. Even though non-assent may be theoretically acceptable within the church, because it is such a closed institutional system, those who disagree do so at risk of their future service in the church.

> *An important difference exists between theoretically disagreeing and practically refusing to obey, between dissenting from some official teaching and actually disobeying it.*

How we achieve truth in the church and consensus around the truth cannot be addressed in any way that would undermine the charismatic authority of the institutional church's teaching office, just as it can be equally said, the charismatic jurisdictional authority cannot be exercised unilaterally apart from the charismatic prophetic authority. However, at the present time the clerical church, especially in its papal and curial expressions, appeals to its charismatic authority of office as justifying why it need not attend to developments in the world that would color its teaching. In this context, one of the greatest tasks facing religious, who are called by the Spirit to signify for the whole church what it means to exercise the charismatic office of prophecy, is to make clear their reservations to the representatives of the clerical church. Thiel notes: "Should magisterial arguments fail to convince, then better, more coherent, traditionally faithful arguments need to be offered by those in the Church who have the ability to justify ecclesial belief." The presentation of "arguments" implies an openness for conversation and dialogue on disputed issues within the church that is called "the People of God." While present ways of functioning in the Roman Curia mitigate against this, Thiel's goal still is something to be desired: "A more dialogical understanding of *ecclesia*, and one more committed to Vatican I's teaching on the complementarity of faith and reason, would not fear public discussion in the Church on how its basic beliefs are logically extended to present circumstances and would be open to the possibility for such dialogue to be the very means of doctrinal development."[15]

Thiel's arguments help us develop our conscience formation, especially when we realize that prophecy sometimes must be exercised through non-assent to the hegemonic positions of the clerical group. His points are less clear regarding when the teaching about which we disagree merits non-submission as well.

Non-assent and dissent usually apply to teaching; non-submission as well as disobedience involve practice, often related to a teaching. An important difference exists between theoretically disagreeing and practically refusing to obey, between dissenting from some official teaching and actually disobeying it. Even raising such a topic, much less acting on it — given the present situation that speaks against dissent and will not tolerate disobedience — creates the potential for serious conflict, including conflict with members of our own religious congregations who have embraced the dominant clerical consciousness. Thus non-assent and non-submission, dissent and disobedience, especially in tightly organized systems that have traditionally demanded unquestioned adherence to teachings and practice, and usually have received it, can create great dissonance externally as well as internally. An awareness of the disruptive consequences of such non-assent and non-submission demands that discussions ordered in this direction should not be undertaken lightly. But the need for such dialogue (a notion at the heart of "evangelical obedience") is critical for our future as religious. Here I agree wholeheartedly with Barbara Fiand:

> Perhaps no other vow stands more stressfully at the crossroads of the "turning point" in our culture's self-understanding than does the vow of obedience. Perhaps also no other evangelical counsel is interpreted still (and especially in our present magisterial setting) with as much dualistic rigidity, resisting the challenge and opportunity of creative rethinking. Perhaps no other virtue is exalted with such absolutism, evoking individualist reactionism in kind and, therefore, closing off all avenues for dialogue and transformation. There seems to be little doubt that obedience in our church is crucified in the intersection of both the archaic vertical and the present-day horizontal modes of relationship. It is the victim par excellence of a hierarchism that cannot as yet yield to the wisdom and sacredness of the community, of a "head" that cannot permit itself to trust its "body" and therefore runs the risk of losing itself in heavenly fantasies of grandeur rather than being rooted in reality, with its feet firmly planted on the earth.[16]

The Role of Non-Submission in the Roman Church

It should be clear that the community called "church" in its Roman Catholic expression is currently conflicted over two counterclaims regarding the role of the Holy Spirit. The first teaches that the Holy Spirit guides the magisterium of the church, which is often unilaterally equated with the papal office and, sometimes, with the bishops if they agree with the papal office; the other teaches that the Holy Spirit also has been poured out within the hearts and consciences of all the baptized.[17] How can the two functions of the Spirit be reconciled in theory as well as in practice and how can the theory and practice be ensured by a law that no longer is recognized as functioning to serve or preserve the clerical caste?

It is critical to realize that the Holy Spirit is the source of power in each of these evangelically grounded ecclesial manifestations. The significance of the Holy Spirit must be recognized not only as the source of "official" teaching but, since there is only one "official church," as the one forming and informing the consciences of the faithful as well. While many aberrations have occurred because of individualistic or subjectivist appeals to "conscience" in ways that equate one's own conscience with the Spirit's will, it must also be recognized that the same occurs when "Matthew 16" subjectively teaches or defines disciplines in ways that have indicated that it has not been open to be taught by the Spirit, much less to learn other ways of interpretation. In matters of such conflict, informed conscience is the way the Spirit enables us to make moral choices regarding the good we will do or the evil we will avoid. Only properly informed consciences are guided by the Holy Spirit. James P. Hanigan writes: "the Holy Spirit is present to and active in the entire process that is conscience."[18]

Consequently, the first obedience due, on the part of the hierarchy as well as the people of God in the Roman Church, is to the Holy Spirit. Neither group has an absolute hegemony on this divine power. From this ultimate authority in the church all other obedience demands mutuality, respect, and trust. Consequently it must be dialogical by nature. When dialogue is not allowed, there can be no freedom or mutuality, much less respect and trust. In such cases *submission is demanded,* even though such submission is called "obedience" by those who demand it. It is for this reason that I chose in this book to refer to the demand for submission as "submission" rather than "obedience." Evangelically ordered relationships grounded in dialogue result in an obedience that is holy; submission without dialogue reflects dynamics that are sinful and abusive. As such, they must be resisted even if they are called "holy obedience.".

Hanigan finds the connection between a well-formed conscience and the Holy Spirit revolving around four interconnected elements. In his mind a Spirit-guided conscience involves (1) a human process that is authoritative, private, and personal in character that (2) takes places within a community's self-understanding or narrative, hence, its absolute character; (3) as it finds itself in some concrete world, hence, its communal character that (4) leads it to be convinced of the moral imperative of acting in some way simply because it is perceived as being true, hence, its objective character.

Each of these elements deserves some further explanation as we discern how our conscience may find the Holy Spirit is leading us to disobey an existing teaching or discipline.

1. A Spirit-guided conscience involves a human process. In the last analysis, any judgment made by individuals or groups on this earth will,

by that fact, represent a human endeavor. While we may believe "God has inspired us," ultimately our choice to act in a certain way will be our judgment, whether individually or collectively. For that judgment and its consequences we must take "full and final responsibility."[19]

Aware that all human judgments that seek to be faithful to the divine vision can suffer from delusion (in which we believe our lie is the truth) or a kind of righteous presumption (in which we cannot be wrong), a healthy dose of humility is required of all parties involved in the conflict. Only when I recognize I might be wrong will I be a fit partner in a dialogue that seeks fidelity to God's plan as its ultimate norm.

2. A Spirit-guided conscience involves discernment within a wider community of conscience. Hanigan notes that, "it is only the narrative context that can either make sense of the disagreement precisely as a disagreement within the community, or reveal that some foreign element with no relation to our life as a people has entered the discussion and changed the very foundations of our life as this particular people." While we must be aware the Spirit works in the leaders of the wider community (i.e., the apostolic charism), these leaders must also acknowledge the Spirit's inspiration at work in the prophetic community as well its other charismatic elements. Hanigan insists:

> If I identify myself with this Spirit-born and Spirit-led community, then I cannot with integrity ignore nor make light of what the community says of itself or of the claims it places upon me. But because the Spirit of Truth is also at work in the individual members of the community, the community, particularly those in authority in the community, has the moral responsibility to listen to and learn from its members. What becomes especially crucial for such a community is to allow room for the prophetic voice witnessing to, calling the community to reform and for a deeper faithfulness to its own identity. Hence, dissenting voices within this Spirit-led community can never be a matter of simple freedom of opinion or the right of individuals to speak their own mind. To speak a word of dissent and challenge to the community called Church is always a prophetic task, a matter of a serious obligation of conscience that calls for a conscientious discernment of the spirit on the part of both the individual and the community.[20]

3. A Spirit-guided conscience cannot be divorced from the world within which its moral decisions are made. "In the year that King Uzziah died," Isaiah experienced the Spirit forming his conscience in a way that redefined for him as sin what previously had been considered by him and his co-religionists as holy. Similarly, as the Pontifical Biblical Commission teaches about "The Interpretation of the Bible in the Church," if we are not aware of the preunderstandings that bring us to the text (in this case, the development of patriarchy in a clerical church), we are no longer interpreting Scripture or tradition in a "Catholic" way.[21]

All judgments as to whether we will or will not do something involve an affirmation of practical reason regarding concrete actions in a complex world. Given this complexity, it will be rare that we can have absolute certitude about decisions we make. It can be presumptuous to equate our historically conditioned decisions to a simple equation of God's will for us, much less others. The most we can say is that "we believe" the Holy Spirit has led us to make this or that choice. The realization of the communally contextualized and historically conditioned world in which we make our choices leads us to Hanigan's fourth point:

4. A Spirit-guided conscience enables us to live the truth of what we are convinced we must be or do. Living "the truth" cannot take place apart from our interaction with others, since truth can only be formed in our consciences through processes of solid informing. In other words, dialogue must define the dynamic.

The statement that we are called to live our truth as the ultimate basis of our moral judgment, i.e., our conscience, upon simple examination, may appear to be arrogant. However, the fact that we can say, with Francis of Assisi, "no man showed me what I ought to do, but the Most High led me to...," ultimately can only arise from a deep religious experience of what we believe to be God's work in our life in a way that also, with Francis, makes us realize we can only obey that which "is not against our conscience." Hanigan calls the accusation identified with such "arrogance" "the prophet's burden." He also notes that, at least in good part, it explains the hostility which is commonly the prophet's lot in life. For who are you, we ask, to claim that you see more and know better than the rest of us?[22] Yet, to submit to something against our conscience and be silent or submissive may be worse than submission to a teaching one perceives to be wrong, especially when the group being critiqued as unfaithful to

God demands silence on our part. Silence in such a matter would involve committing "the unforgivable sin, the sin against the Holy Spirit" insofar as it would represent "the denial of or repudiation of the absolute authority of one's conscience"[23] if we would submit to such abusive power.

Except for theological discussion about statements couched in infallibility, not a lot of theological thought offers us the critical guidance we need in dealing with conscience, especially when that conscience might lead one to disobedience to established teaching in the church that one now determines to be immoral.

Returning to the dispute my own order has with the Vatican over the role of nonordained brothers in positions of highest leadership, the meetings that have taken place have not produced positive fruits. In fact, the rationale for rejecting candidates submitted for acceptance to the ministry of major superior has not included explanations of when the existing norms need not apply. This is understandable, since the institutional teaching would be offering guidelines on how individuals and groups could legitimately disobey its teaching and, therefore, its authority! Thus we must look elsewhere for guidance.

While recognizing that a conscience well-formed in Scriptures and tradition holds primary importance in such matters, in examining official church teaching related to human rights and their violation by governments I find some direction. Here we can consider the current situation in the Roman Church in which its leaders insist on limiting ordination to male celibates even as people are increasingly unable to celebrate the Eucharist on a regular basis.

Referring to the earlier case study about leadership in our Capuchin Franciscan order, our Rule and our conscience as brothers make it clear that all of us who are perpetually professed are equally members of one household. Furthermore we believe that all positions of leadership within our fraternal household should be open to all equally, a position confirmed by the pope almost eight hundred years ago. At the same time, we have taken our vow of obedience to our elected superiors who, in turn promise obedience to the pope of the present day. However, by such a decision from the Vatican, any faithful obedience on our part will find us irreconciled with the decision identified with the one whom our leaders have promised to obey, the pope. But which pope will it be?

At this point it must be remembered that any irreconciliation on the matter comes not from our own ill-will but from the declarations Curia officials themselves have held up to be the norm for action in civil situations. Here and elsewhere, I believe the Vatican's words regarding abortion can be applied to its effort to impose on us its form of clericalization in a way that undermines the right of all friars in perpetual vows to all offices in the order: "If any government does not acknowledge the rights of men or violates them . . . its orders completely lack juridical force," and "a Christian can never conform to a law which is in itself immoral." Since the existing law restricting the major superior in our order to clerics fails to recognize the equal charism of those solemnly professed brothers who are not ordained, such an order lacks juridical force. It seems to me, then, that non-conformity to such an interpretation would allow the group to be free to abide by its own spirit-guided decision.

Applying the Congregation for the Doctrine of the Faith's logic to our situation would not be the only reason for supporting a decision to be non-compliant. Pope Paul VI told religious that, to be properly renewed, we cannot "have any compromise whatsoever with any form of social injustice."[24] In my mind, justice demands that all our perpetually professed brothers be treated as equals and that they have equal access to all resources in the order (including the position of highest superior), be they cleric or lay. Since justice must undergird all law, civil as well as canonical, when the law canonically fails to promote justice (equality in this case), given the absence of solid juridical grounds, a group so affected would be free to return to its own Spirit-guided decision and act on it. Such a move is especially warranted if efforts to redress this wrong have failed to produce the desired results.

The appeal to the Spirit, invoked by the brothers in their previous election, cannot be taken lightly nor can it be reduced to a simple "our" Spirit vs. "their" Spirit difference. The fact that both a group like ours and the decision-makers in the Vatican claim the Spirit's guidance must not be taken lightly, especially when conflicts arise in a noninfallible teaching or discipline such as in a matter like this one. Ultimately any prophetic disobedience to religious or civil authority must arise from a sense of being divinely supported, if not divinely inspired. When the Spirit is invoked within an institution whose leaders believe they are in possession of the Holy Spirit, conflict again will be inevitable. Resolving this conflict demands nuance.

Another situation where this nuance may be necessary involves whether we may now be at a point when noncooperation and even disobedience in the Roman Church is demanded as a way of fulfilling Jesus' demand that we "do" the Eucharist. Despite the dominical demand and church teaching that the Eucharist should be celebrated regularly, especially on Sundays, over half of the Catholics of the world cannot have regular access to the sacrament, in large part because the sacrament of priesthood is limited only to celibate males. The discipline regarding the priesthood must be changed in order to guarantee people's access to the sacrament. The primary right to the Eucharist precedes the secondary right of those who confect the Eucharist.

At a three-day meeting of the presbyterate of a diocese at which I provided some input in late 2002, I had heard from the presiding bishop and many priests that the diocese had 103 parishes and 97 priests. They also told me that their past two actuarial studies regarding priest/parish ratios had both exceeded their "worst-case" scenarios. In addition they noted that, in 2018, less than one generation away, they expected to have 103 parishes and 37 priests.

When the bishop asked my opinion, I said I found all of them submitting to a few in the Vatican in a way that threatened the integrity of their local church. I then applied the principle about procured abortion noted above. I said the people's right to the Eucharist takes precedence over the sex or marital status of the presider. I added that, if I were they, I'd involve the whole diocese in developing principles to prepare noncelibate males for ordination. If adequate notice to the Vatican along with deadlines went unheeded, I argued that they could be justified in proceeding with ordaining qualified married men. The divine demand takes precedence over the human decree. Not one in that presbyterate challenged me. Minimally, their silence can easily be interpreted as support. More frighteningly, they had come to equate submission to an unjust law with obedience itself.

In his preconciliar talk "Do Not Stifle the Spirit," Karl Rahner offered some pointers on "a true and bold interpretation of what *obedience* to the Church really means"[25] that also might guide us in reflecting on whether and how ecclesiastical disobedience might be justified in the church today. Given the fact that the Spirit grounds all charisms in the church, be they the apostolic charism or the prophetic charism or any other, he noted: "The principle which is given to the Church as a concomitant of the love she has to preserve in all her actions lays down that everyone in the Church must follow his own spirit, so long as it is not established beyond all doubt that he is in fact following a pseudospirit."[26] This means that there "are actions which are under God's will, demanded by the conscience of the individual even before the starting signal has been given by the authorities, and furthermore the directions in which these actions tend may be such as are not already approved or established in any positive sense by those authorities."[27] It also means, as may happen when the clerical church insists on some faulty teaching or unjust discipline, that we have the courage to resist them in the hope that this rejection will be a means of "rousing the official Church to perform its function"[28] more justly and more inclusively.

The fact that both a group like ours and the decision-makers in the Vatican claim the Spirit's guidance must not be taken lightly.

It is the mandate of all religious concerned about maintaining fidelity to their charism to find ways to ensure its authentic expression in an institutional church whose leaders often seem more intent on maintaining their clerical model of the church than a charismatic one. Joan Chittister notes that we have inherited a form of religious life in which great attention was "given to the definitions of types and distinctions between orders, [so] commitment to religious life gradually became thought of more as a canonical form of life than a charismatic form of life, more as a set of rules to be followed than a set of ideals to be sought."[29] Consequently contemporary religious — who find themselves and their charisms compromised because of the canonical context in which they are told to express them — must undertake their own examination to determine when and how canonically justified dynamics may be undermining the essential integrity of the charism and then decide how to act. They must develop their own rationales, based on their founders' approach, to justify whether or not they can disagree and in what circumstances they can loyally and faithfully disagree. A Franciscan approach may not be the Benedictine way.

As I noted previously, Chittister's own community, the Erie Benedictines, realized it needed to discern whether it would submit to a unilateral order from the Roman Curia demanding that she not give a speech in Dublin in 2001. Its discernment not to act on the demand was made almost unanimously, with one dissenting voice. Its understanding of obedience demanded an active form of dialogue on a subject between the parties involved. As Christine Vladimiroff, O.S.B., prioress of the sisters, said in a press statement: "There is a fundamental difference in the understanding of obedience in the monastic tradition and that which is being used by the Vatican."[30] Ultimately, each religious congregation must make such deliberations come alive in light of their self-understanding and their charism.[31] These also must take place in an obedience that is "holy."

It is important to remember that many people who have been convinced they were inspired by the Spirit were suppressed or censored by the authorities. Only later would the very members representing the institution that persecuted them determine them to be saints. Often the attestation of their holiness was not identified only in their vision, but also the tenacity of their inspiration which they honored through their resistance to the highest church authorities. One of the most recent examples of this is the Australian "Blessed" Mary McKillop. What is most remarkable about her, Robert Ellsberg writes in his popular *All Saints: Daily Reflections on Saints, Prophets, and Witnesses for Our Time,* is not so much the charitable work by which she expressed her faith as the utterly uncharitable treatment she received at the hands of many priests and prelates in her time. Indeed, Mary McKillop might serve as the patron saint of all who have suffered the petty persecution of narrow-minded religious authorities, convinced they are acting in the place of God. That Mary remained free of bitterness, despite her ordeals, is considerable evidence of her sanctity and sufficient cause for honor.[32]

How the Charism of Our Founders Was Ensured in Face of the Hierarchy

I am aware that not all Franciscans share the same assumptions about our founders, Francis and Clare of Assisi, and I discovered that this was the case when I talked publicly about them and their spirituality some years ago. I had been asked to give a presentation at a suburban, middle-class parish in the greater Milwaukee area during Lent as part of an overall parish reflection on the notion of conversion. I decided to explain Francis's experience of conversion and its implications for today. About a hundred people attended, including eight women from a traditional Franciscan congregation.

I used Francis's own words detailing his initial conversion experience. He describes it in his "Testament," which he authored shortly before his death. He begins it all with the words: "The Lord granted to me, Brother Francis, to begin to do penance in this way. While I was in sin, it seemed very bitter to me to see lepers. And the Lord Himself led me among them and I had mercy upon them. And when I left them that which seemed bitter to me was changed into sweetness of soul and body; and afterward I lingered a little and left the world."[33]

I began by describing the notion of "the world" as Francis understood it; this involved a degree of social analysis. Then I explained who represented "lepers" at the time of Jesus and what happened to those called "lepers" in his world and the world of Assisi twelve hundred years later. At the end of my talk, the nuns and the others immediately left the church for the cookies and punch in the church vestibule. When I got there only two young couples who were social workers excitedly came up to me making all sorts of connections. With evident disappointment, a woman approached me and asked: "Why didn't you talk about the animals?" I prudently declined to answer. At this critical time, when we find our church "falling into ruin," my own opinion is that we Franciscans and Clares have a greater urgency to probe what our charism invites us to be and do than to dwell on what I would call religious sentimentalism. However, the point is, within my own Franciscan community, there is not general agreement about the charisms of our founders.

In the previous chapters I noted how their image of living as "pilgrims and strangers in this world" might serve as a segue to a deeper

understanding of being in exile. I also noted that the crisis that characterizes the present state of the Roman Church in the more developed world
indicates a great need for radical structural transformation. No matter
what words we use to describe the present state of institutional Catholicism, we know there are problems. Consequently, asking the indulgence
of those not sharing our charism, I conclude this chapter with what I consider a "Franciscan" way to address the reality of being in a church that
all can see is falling into ruin.

After Francis's conversion experience with the leper, Brother Thomas
of Celano, his first biographer, writes (in the flowery style of that era's
hagiographers):

> Changed now perfectly in heart and soon to be changed in body
> too, he was walking one day near the church of St. Damian, which
> had nearly fallen to ruin and was abandoned by everyone. Led by
> the Spirit, he went in and fell down before the crucifix in doubt and
> humble supplication; and smitten by unusual visitations, he found
> himself other than he had been when he entered. While he was thus
> affected, something unheard of before happened to him: the painted
> image of Christ crucified moved its lips and spoke. Calling him by
> name it said: "Francis, go, repair my house, which, as you see, is
> falling completely to ruin."[34]

Despite conditions in society and the institutional church in the late
1100s and early 1200s, Francis never imagined leaving the institution,
despite the power of a Pope like Innocent III nor the abuse of power he
witnessed in various bishops and priests. In fact, as the great Franciscan
writer Thadée Matura has emphasized, Francis demanded "a scrupulous
obedience to ecclesiastical prescriptions."[35] Serene in the wisdom of knowing he couldn't change its bureaucracy, he determined that the best way
of "repairing the house" would be by courageously creating an alternative
community within the institution, a household of brothers, and by supporting Clare in her new household of sisters at San Damiano. Together
they would inspire an alternative community of religious and laypeople
who would, by their refusal to bear arms, do much to bring about needed
change in feudal society. I will argue that, while Francis's approach may
not have changed society as such nor reformed the institutional church

per se, it did breathe into the body of Christ a new expression of the Spirit that represented a life-giving alternative.

With Clare, however, her "obedience" was more nuanced, for she refused to submit to the pope even as she declared her loyalty to him. Since her way of dealing with Rome in conflicts expressed itself differently from Francis's, I want to show how she too serves as a model of resistance for us when we find ourselves at odds with the ways of Rome.

Francis's Alternative "House" to the Other "House" Falling into Ruin

In order to recognize how Francis's call might have an echo in our church, we need to examine more deeply the kind of entrenched and institutionalized power system within the "house" that Francis felt himself divinely mandated to repair.[36]

The first chapter showed that, as part of the "Constantinianization of the Church," the first pope called "Innocent" declared that the Holy Spirit could be invoked only through the power of the hierarchy. Later, Pope Innocent III firmly believed the papacy's role was to rule theocratically. He was to be the supreme power at the head of a hierarchy of vassal states. In fulfilling this goal he proved to be very successful.

Arnaldo Fortini writes: "His success had exceeded his every aspiration, since kings and emperors were now coming to prostrate themselves humbly at his feet, receive their crowns from him, renounce their secular prerogatives, and obey him without argument. In truth, he was by now able to consider himself the lord of all, who at will controlled the world,"[37] (the world, of course, being the world known to Europeans at that time). He evidenced this power by humbling Otto IV on October 4, 1209, refusing to permit the emperor to cross the Tiber into Rome. The emperor obeyed the pope. This same year Francis and his first followers received approval for their "gospel" way of life — from none other than this arguably theocratic Innocent III.

Within the world's notion of power, where people were divided between the haves and the have-nots, the *majores* and the *minores*, even higher and lower clergy, Francis adopted the name "minor" for himself and those who would follow his way of living in the world. In the institutional church's *modus operandi*, where form followed function, part of its ruin could be traced to the way so many men coveted and clung to prelacies. Francis resisted these temptations. Responding to a bishop who suggested his followers become bishops, Francis reportedly declared:

> "Lord, my brothers are called *minors* so that they will not presume to become greater. Their vocation teaches them to remain in a lowly station and to follow the footsteps of the humble Christ, so that in the end they may be exalted above the rest in the sight of the saints. If," he said, "you want them to bear fruit for the church of God, hold them and preserve them in the station to which they have been called, and bring them back to a lowly station, even if they are unwilling. I pray you, therefore, Father, that you by no means permit them to rise to any prelacy, lest they become prouder rather than poorer and grow arrogant toward the rest."[38]

In the context of a church and society defined by *majores* and *minores*, Francis not only immersed himself in the Holy Spirit as the great equalizer; he also found in the relationships within the triune God a model of equality that he envisioned for his new household within the old "house" that was falling into ruin. In one of his most-used references from John's Gospel, he showed eloquently and clearly how his followers — indeed all the faithful — must be grounded in this triune God. For instance, in his "Letter to All the Faithful," he wrote:

> And upon all men and women, if they have done these things and have persevered to the end, *the Spirit of the Lord will rest* (cf. Isa. 11:2) and He will make His home and *dwelling among them* (cf. John 14:23). They will be children of the heavenly Father (cf. Matt. 5:45) whose works they do. And they are spouses, brothers, and mothers of our Lord Jesus Christ (cf. Matt. 12:50). We are spouses when the faithful is joined to Jesus Christ by the Holy Spirit. We are brothers when we do *the will* of His *Father Who* is in heaven (cf. Matt. 12:50). [We are] mothers when we carry Him in our heart and body (cf. 1 Cor. 6:20) through love and a pure and sincere conscience; we give birth to Him through [His] holy manner of working which should shine before others as an example.[39]

Some scholars, like Engelbert Grau and Kajetan Esser, insist Francis never set out to reform the church. Others, like Paul Sabbatier, say that he and his evangelical vision were co-opted by the institutional church. Rather than side with one position or the other, I believe Francis's way must be seen as a both/and approach, representing a new way of being church that effectively subverted the arrogant model of church prevalent in his day. In my heart of hearts, I want to believe that this kind of subversive reform might still be a model from which we might learn volumes.

We learn a bit of Francis's own way of offering an alternative way of life when we recall how some of his followers grew tired of his austerity and tried to change his direction. Not able to persuade him to change, they sought help from the hierarchy, especially Cardinal Hugolino, the future Pope Gregory IX. Together they worked hard to persuade Francis to join one of the traditional religious orders. Again Francis resisted. Holding his ground before the cardinal and his brothers-in-conspiracy, the *Legend of Perugia* says Francis declared:

> "My brothers, my brothers, God called me to walk in the way of humility and showed me the way of simplicity.... The Lord has told me that he wanted to make a new fool of me in the world and God does not want to lead us by any other knowledge than that. God will use your personal knowledge and your wisdom to confound you; he has policemen to punish you, and I put my trust in him. Then to your shame you will return to your first state, whether you like it or not!" The cardinal, dumbfounded, kept silence, and all the brothers were gripped by fear.[40]

Though Francis never seemed to suffer any serious problem in fulfilling his dream within the institutional church, we cannot conclude that Francis rejected any resistance or was clerically codependent if church leaders had insisted on something against his conscience. In his own Rule. which we follow to this day, he clearly establishes the line of authority in the order squarely within the Roman system: "The rule and life of the Friars Minor is this: to observe the holy Gospel of our Lord Jesus Christ by living in obedience, without anything of their own, and in chastity. Brother Francis promises obedience and reverence to the Lord Pope Honorius and his canonically elected successors and to the Roman Church. And let the other brothers be bound to obey Brother Francis and his successors."[41]

This passage is clear: Francis's First Order followers must obey the head of the order, who, in turn, obeys the pope. With this hierarchical understanding of obedience, any obedience we vow to the pope as Franciscans is observed indirectly, through obedience to our superiors. However, Francis writes in the same Rule, approved by Rome, that when we feel in conscience we cannot obey, we are no longer bound to what is demanded: "I strictly command them to obey their ministers in all those things which they have promised the Lord to observe and which are not against [their] consciences and our Rule."[42] Conscience, then as now, is the ultimate criterion for all obedience.

Given the various parts of the Rule related to our obedience to superiors and their obedience to the pope, it is clear that there will be times when the two forms of obedience might conflict. How can this to be resolved? By a simple submission to the prophetic charism or the apostolic charism? I don't think such a simple solution would be faithful to our Scriptures or our tradition. To give us a different approach regarding dissent and disobedience, we turn to Clare of Assisi.

Clare's Model of Resistance: A Feminine Way to "Repair the House"

Two years after Francis received formal approval for his way of life, under the patronage of Bishop Guido, Clare began translating his vision into feminine form. Before her family discovered what she had done and insisted on her return, Francis escorted her to the sanctuary of a nearby Benedictine convent. From there she moved to Sant'Angelo di Panzo near the Carceri, a favored place of retreat for Francis. Sixteen days after Clare left her house, her sister Agnes joined her, and shortly after they moved to San Damiano, where Clare remained for the rest of her life.

Three years after the foundation of Clare's community, the Fourth Lateran Council decreed that any new religious communities not yet approved must adopt the rule of an established order. Because the "form of life" written for her by Francis lacked official approval, the "Ladies of San Damiano," as they were called, were given the Benedictine Rule, and with this assignment of a non-Franciscan Rule began a series of conflicts between Clare and the male authorities in Rome.

The Benedictine Rule allowed for monasteries to own property.[43] Clare wanted the "privilege of poverty" enjoyed by the brothers. This meant her sisters could neither individually nor collectively claim ownership of property. Clare appealed for this *privilegium paupertatis* to Innocent III. In this case "it worked; with later pontiffs, questions arose," Ingrid Peterson writes. They weren't "resolved until her death bed."[44] When Innocent died in 1216, the cardinal protector of her order was Cardinal Hugolino. In 1218, following the Lateran Council's decree about no new Rules, he once more imposed on the Poor Ladies the Benedictine Rule; to it he added a "form of life" he thought adapted to her situation. Since this did not include the poverty privilege, Clare sought it again. Hugolino did not want to reinstate it, but Clare remained steadfast. The "Most High," God's Spirit, had revealed to her that she should live evangelically in poverty. Her arguments prevailed; Hugolino acceded. However, when Hugolino later became Pope Gregory IX, he again tried to pressure Clare to change her course. Believing corporate poverty might prove too difficult for the community, he urged her to accept possessions. Again Clare resisted his proposal and, again, he relented. In 1228, he reiterated Innocent's decision and reapproved the *privilegium paupertatis.*

On the surface things seemed to go well. However, Clare still chafed under the Benedictine Rule, and she wanted her own. Having prevailed in 1219 when Cardinal Hugolino tried to impose on her a way of life foreign to her vision, Clare faced another hurdle later in 1245. At that time a new pope, Innocent IV, unilaterally repealed the privilege of poverty and conferred another Rule on the San Damiano group, an action Clare could not accept. In conscience she and her sisters could not obey a papal rule that undermined what she considered a mandate from "the Most High." So strong was their reaction that Innocent withdrew his Rule. At this time she decided at last to compose her own Rule.

The Rule of St. Clare, as history now calls it, was approved by the cardinal protector of the order at the time (later Pope Alexander IV) on September 16, 1252. However, Clare wanted yet more: approval by Pope Innocent IV himself. Even as she lay on her deathbed, Clare persisted in this conviction of conscience. In face of her insistence and persistence, Innocent relented. He journeyed to San Damiano and gave verbal acceptance to the Rule she herself had written. The bull making legal her Rule was issued on August 9, 1253, and hand-delivered by a friar on August 10. Clare died the next day, August 11, now her feast day.

Approval of Clare's Rule was a canonical milestone, for it was the first time a Rule written by a woman for women was approved by the highest Roman authority. Aidan McGraith notes:

> Alexander IV, who had given his approval to the Rule while the Cardinal Protector, spoke of her quite clearly as a true foundress, "the first and solid foundation of this great religious way of life." As a result, her sisters came to be known by her name: although St. Francis had always referred to them as "Poor Ladies," after the death of Clare, they became known universally as the Order of Saint Clare or simply as the Poor Clares.[45]

All the while Clare lived according to her Rule, without its being approved by Rome, she promised "obedience and reverence to the Lord Pope Innocent and to his canonically elected successors, and to the Roman Church,"[46] in the Rule itself! I am convinced that she believed she was obeying, even as she refused to submit. That she knew the difference should make us ask: "How could she have been so adamant in resisting the earlier rules popes and their representative tried to force on her?" The answer seems simple, if we read what she wrote at the beginning of her Rule: "The form of life of the Order of the Poor Sisters which the Blessed Francis established, is this: to observe the holy Gospel of Our Lord Jesus Christ, by living in obedience, without anything of one's own, and in chastity."[47] The Gospel's mandate trumped any fiat of the pope. Obedience to her divine inspiration preceded her human submission to a pope. In her mind the way she and her sisters would "repair the house" could only be by radical observance of the evangelical poverty of Jesus.[48]

While Clare's dissent over a rule defined much of her life, especially her latter years, she resisted Rome's encroachments at other times as well. In 1230, her friend Gregory IX issued a decree making it practically impossible for the friars to preach God's word to the sisters. Clare became so angry that she fired the friars. More defiantly, she decided to do what women of her era resorted to do in the face of brute male power: she began to pray and fast. Clare's mode of fasting, Caroline Walker Bynum writes, was not just a pious activity; it was active resistance, a "holy anorexia."[49] This form of resistance demonstrates that hunger strikes did not begin with Gandhi. As he had done earlier in response to Clare's resistance to any undermining of her "Privilege of Poverty," now, with her refusal to accept food, Gregory relented.

It is important to note nowadays how at that time in the institutional church, such forms of debate and disagreement, and even the kind of disobedience evidenced by Clare, were not labeled "disloyalty." Then, unlike now, when a form of real dialogue still existed in the ecclesiastical system, such expressions of resistance to the institutional mandates often were acknowledged to represent concrete manifestations of fidelity to the Spirit working in one's life, despite institutional differences. Indeed, it was the very fact of her *resistance* that Clare showed popes and protectors regarding the matter of the *privilegium paupertatis* that was considered in her beatification process as concrete evidence of her *Spirit*-based grounding and holiness.[50]

In her writings Clare also sought to ground her order in an experience of a communitarian, interpersonal God. She linked her sisters' very identity to their membership in the household of God. Invariably she refers to her followers as "sister," "spouse," and even "mother." Such images also are found in her Rule. In one place she quotes from the "Form of Life" Francis gave her and her sisters:

> Since by divine inspiration you have made yourselves daughters and servants of the most high King, the heavenly Father, and have taken the Holy Spirit as your spouse, choosing to live according to the perfection of the holy Gospel, I resolve and promise for myself and for my brothers always to have that same loving care and special solicitude for you as [I have] for them.[51]

Like Francis, Clare always insisted on being submissive to Roman authorities and being loyal to the pope and his representatives. Yet her biography makes it clear that her way of expressing that submission and loyalty was manifested in nontraditional ways of obedience, especially when the papacy and hierarchy tried to pressure her to deviate from what she believed to be her divinely inspired vocation. Hers was a calling not to be defined by humans; she was ultimately responsible to her conscience and her God.

In that she would not accept Rome's demands as to how she would constitute her order, I believe that it's important to note that Clare would not resist the hierarchy without Francis's support. Although she did not need it, it seems he lent her his full backing when she discerned the need to dissent. Possibly expecting she would have trouble from the hierarchy after he died, Francis wrote in his "Last Will" to Clare: "Keep close watch over yourselves so that you never abandon it [the holy life of poverty] through the teaching or advice of *anyone*."[52] I believe that, while Francis may never personally have had any significant differences with Rome, these words of Francis to Clare make it clear that room exists for a Franciscan model of non-assent and non-submission.

Principles for Repairing the House Falling into Ruin

Given this historical background, we now can ask: What can we learn from Francis's and Clare's response to what Celano calls the "deadly disease" that afflicted the whole church,[53] especially in the way these two witnessed to their evangelical spirituality within its institutional expression? First, a Franciscan style of resistance places much greater stress on alternative models of what it means to be "house" than on direct dissent and disobedience. "But," one may ask, "what happens when it comes to the point when dissent and resistance seem to be the only recourse people of integrity can take?" My response is that I think it's important to be *very* sure that such a point of no return has actually been reached. We should always be open to the question: Could *we* be wrong? Where are our blinders? When we are not open to considering the possibility we may be wrong, the possibility exists that *our* ideology may have overtaken our own passion for truth. However, given such caution, if events find us at a point when we discern no alternative, I believe Francis and Clare still offer us some guidelines.

Francis's approach to obedience contextualized it in fidelity to the clerical leaders of the Roman Church but from *within* a community whose members would obey their ministers and, above all, with conscience as primary authority. Within this understanding, I'd like to offer eight principles for non-assent and non-submission to keep us faithful to the nonviolent, ecclesial way of Francis and Clare. The first four flow from their common charism, the fifth and sixth arise from Francis's unique approach, and the final two are derived from Clare herself.

1. In reference to the very nature and identity of our life, *no human authority on earth can undermine what must reflect our grounding in the Holy Spirit.* Where human authority, such as that of the pope, is to be part of decision-making in the essentials, it also must be willing to be grounded in what this Spirit authenticates. Thus Francis wrote in his final "Testament": "And after the Lord gave me brothers, no one showed me what I should do, but the Most High Himself revealed to me that I should live according to the form of the Holy Gospel. And I had this written down simply and in a few words and the Lord Pope confirmed it for me."[54] For her part Clare wrote her sister Agnes at the very time Agnes was resisting a pope's efforts to mitigate her understanding of poverty: "If anyone would tell you something else or suggest something which would hinder your perfection or seem contrary to your divine vocation, even though you must respect him, do not follow his counsel."[55] The Holy Spirit must ground all authority in the church. This Spirit must be obeyed.

2. *We must be convinced that whatever we do is grounded in the Holy Spirit, not our own spirit.* In this, our goal should be to strive to live under the same "Spirit of the Lord" and its "holy manner of working"[56] that guided Francis and Clare. This Spirit is the ultimate authority not only in the order, as in all congregations, but in the church itself. All must be submissive to this Spirit who breathes in the whole church and its members as it wills. Aware of this, Hanigan offers us an important caveat: "Those who seek to be faithful to Christ can never invoke the Spirit or their experience of the Spirit as evidence that the judgments of their consciences are objectively right; they can only appeal to the Spirit for evidence that those judgments have been conscientious."[57] This is a critical, humbling distinction.

Francis wanted his followers to humbly submit to this spiritual basis for their charismatic presence in the church. In what could possibly be a reference to the very human ways of the Roman Curia, Thomas of Celano writes: "With God," Francis said, "there is no respect of persons, and the minister general of the order, the Holy Spirit, rests equally upon the poor and the simple." He wanted this thought inserted into his rule, but since it was already approved by papal bull, this could not be done.

3. Where the first two principles converge, another flows as a consequence: *an ecclesially informed conscience (whether personal, communal, or congregational) must be the ultimate norm to characterize our obedience to all legitimate authority.* As we have seen, Francis wrote in his Rule that the

individual members of the order were under the jurisdiction of the minister general; he, in turn, was under obedience to the pope. But he added: "Therefore I strictly command them to obey their ministers in all those things which they have promised the Lord to observe and which are not against [their] conscience and our Rule."[58] The potential for conflict is inherent in the two objects of the friars' obedience, which must ultimately be in accord with their consciences: their ministers and, through the highest minister, the minister general, to the pope.

It is true that our evangelical obedience must be ecclesially, and even ecclesiastically, informed; yet it is equally true this conscience must be formed according to the four elements discussed by Hanigan that I noted above. Such an informed conscience must define "obedience" for the friars.

4. The fourth principle results from all the above: *where differences exist between leaders of the institutional church and the members, any dissent must be grounded in authentic discernment.* Hanigan also says the "various spiritual traditions of discernment of spirits in the Catholic community have been largely carried through history in religious orders and congregations, in the experiences of saints and mystics, for all of whom a docility of the human spirit, and so of obedience to authority, was of major importance." He also insists that "the obedience they recommended and practiced was never in the interests of social conformity or the avoidance of conflict" or in a way that denied what they believed "the Holy Spirit had taught them personally." Given the fact that the obedience they urged was in the interests of freedom in the Spirit, he concludes that their approach now finds us at another point in history:

> It seems likely that we can no longer think easily or speak readily in terms of blind obedience or of conforming without question our minds and hearts to the official teaching of Church authorities in all its aspects. For reasons of both practical experience and theoretical insight, that road is now closed to many of us. . . . We have, unfortunately, too often expressed this basic experience of disagreement or dis-ease with official teaching as a conflict between two authorities, the authority of conscience and the authority of the Church hierarchy. But . . . there is only one authority, the authority of the Holy Spirit, the author of life in the Church and in the members of the Church, to which we owe allegiance.[59]

All involved must make sure their process of discernment checks against ideology, delusion, deception, distortion, and righteousness. Time-honored principles of discernment must be ensured, which assume teaching as well as learning at the heart of the discussions that take place between individuals and groups in disagreement.

5. *When dissent is deemed necessary, our approach should be respectful and courteous as we continually request dialogue about our differences.* Aidan McGraith writes that just because Rome approved Clare's Rule it should not be viewed in terms of a conflict that Clare won. Rather, what happened "in the approval of the Rule of St. Clare is an example of the dialogue that takes place between charism and the institution. In that dialogue, it became evident that what Clare was proposing was not simply something of her own, a purely personal idea or inclination, but a gift from God to the whole Church."[60] Respect for those in the hierarchy we oppose should define our stance as we explain our positions. Every creature, including those whose positions we feel harm the church, especially the clergy, has a claim on our courtesy. Aware that the clergy may be sinning, Francis pointed to what they represented rather than where they stumbled. In his "Testament" he wrote that his faith in priests was such that, even if they persecuted him, he'd keep coming back; in fact he did not want to consider the sin that might be in them, because he saw himself subservient to them. He did this because of their role in making present the eucharistic presence "of the Most High Son of God in this world" through "His Most holy Body and Blood which they receive and which they alone administer to others."[61]

6. Within this respectful and courteous stance, *we should never hesitate to speak our understanding of truth clearly and charitably to our authorities.* To live in truth is the goal of all moral discernment. Practicing this truth takes place in the power of the Holy Spirit under whom both of us (those with the charism of authority and those with the charism of prophecy) should be obedient. In all things the guiding norm should be to practice the truth in love in order to build up the body of Christ. Thus Paul wrote to the Church at Ephesus: "But speaking the truth in love, we must grow up in every way into him who is the head, into Christ, from whom the whole body, joined and knit together by every ligament with which it is equipped, as each part is working properly, promotes the body's growth in building itself up in love" (Eph. 4:15). Hanigan reminds us that "it is the

Holy Spirit that sets us free by teaching us the truth." And he adds that: "The loyalty of our individual consciences, and the loyalty of the Church as a whole, is a loyalty to the truth, a truth which neither conscience nor the community creates, but a truth given to us as gift and responsibility, discovered by us, calling for our assent."[62]

7. In the event that decrees and decisions critically undermine our life and the life of the body, *when we discern the need for Spirit-grounded non-compliance and non-submission, it should be nourished by prayer and fasting.* When we find ourselves believing we are being led by the Spirit to do or not do something in the church that finds us at odds with its leaders (who are demanding the opposite because they also believe they are led by the Spirit), we are brought into the heart of claims and counterclaims with the resulting conflict over the issue of the exercise of power and jurisdiction in the Church. In face of such overwhelming conflicts, prayer and fasting may be the only resort left to keep our minds clear, our hearts steadfast, and our souls grounded in the Spirit. Such prayer and fasting for us, as it was for Clare, may also be concrete forms of protest that witness publicly as a clear and concrete sign of the conviction of our conscience.

8. Finally, *we should be willing to joyfully bear any cost that may be incurred by our act(s) of resistance* that may result from the other's counterresistance. Increasingly I am convinced that joy stands not only as the inevitable sign of one's experience of the Spirit; it also characterizes the character of the heart willing to suffer all in order to be faithful. In this joy we can have no greater example than the first disciple of Francis, Clare of Assisi herself. She was willing to die joyfully outside of obedience to the pope, convinced of the Spirit's support for her decision. At this point, our only dream is that what happened to her will happen to us: Rome relented.

In concluding that there is a need for non-assent and even non-submission vis-à-vis those ecclesiastical mandates considered wrong or unjust, we can find joy as well as courage from the Vatican's own nurturing words of support for those who would resist other human rules that undermine the dignity of people. The 1971 Synod of Bishops declared that "within the church, rights must be preserved. No one should be deprived of his ordinary rights because he is associated with the Church in one way or another."[63] Furthermore, arguing why people must reject decisions of governments that make rules based on the denial of basic rights, the Congregation for the Doctrine of the Faith stated:

Following one's conscience in obedience to the law of God is not always the easy way. One must not fail to recognize the weight of the sacrifices and the burdens which it can impose. Heroism is sometimes called for in order to remain faithful to the requirements of the Divine law. Therefore we must emphasize that the path of true progress of the human person passes through this constant fidelity to a conscience maintained in uprightness and truth; and we must exhort all those who are able to do so to lighten the burdens still crushing so many men and women, families and children, who are placed in situations to which in human terms there is no solution.[64]

Conclusion

Originally this book ended with the sentence above. However, the day I finished reading the page proofs, I felt it would be incomplete if it ended there. It seemed cold and impersonal; it didn't offer enough hope.

That night a friend from the Twin Cities called. We started talking about "covenants." Our conversation made me realize that true covenants and vows assume fidelity on the part of all parties involved — to promises made to live evangelically. This concept grounds all authentic obedience.

In our tradition we make vows in the context of covenantal fidelity: because of God's promises we make our own; we make our commitment convinced of God's abiding promise of "eternal life." Furthermore, all about this way of obedience to the covenant is anchored in dialogue.

When I entered the Capuchin Franciscan order in 1959, the notion of dialogue at the heart of obedience was incomprehensible to me. To obey simply meant I must follow the orders of those who were part of what I've called the "Church of Matthew 16": Jesus gave all authority to Peter and, by extension, to the popes. They shared their full authority with the canonically elected superiors and priests in leadership. I embraced the notion without reservation; I even wrote a book on how we Franciscans should follow without question what the popes said we should do.[65]

Only when I had a jarring experience in the way some of these clerics exercised that authority did I face a "crisis" in obedience. My father had begun a long dying process. For the sake of their tradition of control, they were unwittingly violating God's command that I honor him with home visits (Matt. 15:1–9), even though my Capuchin brother, Dan, could do so. They even said it was God's will that I not visit him. When he suffered a stroke, which ultimately led to his death, I was allowed to go home. On the day of his burial, when I saw some of the priests coming to return me to the seminary, I thought to myself: "I will go back to your seminary, I will submit to every one of your rules, but never again will I give you or any other human being or institution the power to control my mind."

Every covenant with God involves a mutual fidelity that grounds all involved in freedom. This demands informed consciences as well as dialogue when there are differences. Only such a mutual stance of listening, freely exercised and embraced, is holy; it can never be coerced. If one part of a covenant demands submission contrary to an informed conscience, especially when that one is in authority and refuses dialogue, such cannot be called evangelical or "holy" obedience; rather it reveals a kind of control that can be effected only through submission. To violate one's conscience by submitting to such abuse of authority undermines the integrity of covenantal fidelity. Thus, if the relationship between the authority and the subject of that authority is not dialogical, respectful, and mutual, it will be neither holy authority nor holy obedience. Rather it will reflect dynamics of control expressed in abuse, on the one hand, and submission on the other. In the process all parties will be dehumanized and, therefore, less graced; furthermore, a truly *evangelical* obedience will be given lip-service rather than witness.

If, in such a situation, submission still is ordered, let it be called what it is: submission. Then the vow of true evangelical obedience will be honored — for the good of the church. Thus preserved, all involved can celebrate an obedience that will be truly holy. Unless and until such authentic obedience can be celebrated, we will need prophetic voices to name its aberration as "sin" — whether it be in empire or *ekklēsía* — and to invite to conversion those who have violated their God-given office.

Notes

Introduction / Prophetic Proclamation in a Church Constitutively Clerical

1. Key among these materials were talks I gave to the Canadian Religious Conference in the 1980s. These were condensed into a six-part series entitled *Transforming Religious Life*, produced by Ave Maria Press. The series is now out of print.

2. Patricia F. Walter, O.P., "Religious Life in Church Documents," *Review for Religious* 51 (1992): 552. I am indebted to Sister Patricia for her overview. It has helped form the next paragraphs of this chapter.

3. Ibid., 553.

4. Ibid., 555, referring to nos. 13, 16–22, and 25.

5. Congregation for Religious and for Secular Institutes, "Religious Life and Human Promotion," 1978, 27.

6. Walter, "Religious Life in Church Documents," 556.

7. Pope John Paul II, *Vita Consecrata,* Apostolic Exhortation on the Consecrated Life, March 25, 1996, 84, in *Consecrated Life* (Boston: Pauline Books & Media, 1996), 137.

8. Ibid., 138.

9. According to the instruction from the congregation controlling religious and secular institutes, "consecrated persons and their institutions are called to give proof of unity without disagreement with the magisterium of the church." "Starting Afresh from Christ: A Renewed Commitment to Consecrated Life in the Third Millennium," *Origins* 32 (2002): 143.

10. Paul Tillich, *The Dynamics of Faith* (New York: Harper, 1957), 72.

11. Sister Kathleen Pruitt, C.S.J.P., "To Serve as Prophets of Hope in This Time, This Place," August 18, 2002, *Origins* 32 (2002): 231.

12. Sandra Schneiders, I.H.M., *Finding the Treasure: Locating Catholic Religious Life in a New Ecclesial and Cultural Context* (New York: Paulist Press, 2000), 156.

13. Notes distributed at the 1989 Louisville assembly.

14. David Nygren and Miriam Ukeritis, "Future of Religious Orders in the United States," Executive Summary, *Origins* 22 (1992): 259.

15. Ibid., 260.

16. Ibid., 264.

17. Ibid., 272.

18. International Forum of Religious for Global Solidarity, "Global Challenges to Religious," CSR Quest Publication 126 (Colombo, Sri Lanka: Centre for Society & Trends and Religion, 1994),17.

19. Schneiders, *Finding the Treasure*, 327.

20. Joan Chittister, O.S.B., *The Fire in These Ashes: A Spirituality of Contemporary Religious Life* (Kansas City, Mo.: Sheed & Ward, 1995), 62.

21. Richard Rohr, "Religious Life Has Been Totally Co-opted," *National Catholic Reporter,* March 8, 2002.

22. Morris L. West, *The Shoes of the Fisherman* (New York: William Morrow, 1963), 270.

23. Saul Alinsky, *Rules for Radicals: A Practical Primer for Realistic Radicals* (New York: Random House, 1971), 87–88.

24. For a history of the tripartite ordering in the Roman Catholic Church, see Peter J. Drilling, "The Priest, Prophet and King Trilogy: Elements of Its Meaning in *Lumen Gentium* and for Today," *Église et Théologie* 19 (1988): 179–206.

25. A quarter of a century ago, the Salesian Scripture scholar Francis J. Moloney wrote *Disciples and Prophets: A Biblical Model for the Religious Life* (New York: Crossroad, 1981). His approach is more inspirational and stresses the vows.

26. Schneiders, *Finding the Treasure,* 150–51

27. Diarmuid O'Murchu, M.S.C., *Religious Life: A Prophetic Vision: Hope and Promise for Tomorrow* (Notre Dame, Ind.: Ave Maria, 1991).

Chapter 1 / An Overview of Prophecy in Scripture and Tradition

1. The "Solomonic" ideology that pervaded Israel in a way that demanded prophecy has been well outlined by Walter Brueggemann in *The Prophetic Imagination,* fully revised and updated (Minneapolis: Fortress, 2001), 31ff.

2. In this book I usually refer to the Southern Kingdom as Judah. However, I also call it Israel, despite the fact that the Northern Kingdom was called by that name. When I refer to Judah as Israel I am referring to Israel as the community of God's people that became institutionalized into two kingdoms, Israel and Judah.

3. Tamara C. Eskenazi, "Exile and the Dreams of Return," *Currents in Theology and Mission* 17 (1990): 195.

4. Joseph Blenkinsopp, *The Men Who Spoke Out: The Old Testament Prophets* (London: Darton Longman and Todd, 1969), 103.

5. Abraham J. Heschel, *The Prophets II* (New York: Harper Torchbooks, 1971), 262.

6. Brueggemann, *The Prophetic Imagination,* 31.

7. Alan Wolfe, "The New Politics of Inequality," Op-Ed Piece, *New York Times,* September 22, 1999.

8. Brueggemann, *The Prophetic Imagination,* 3.

9. O'Murchu, *Religious Life,* quoting Richard Endres, 36–37.

10. Ronald E. Clements, "Max Weber, Charisma and Biblical Prophecy," in *Prophecy and Prophets,* ed. Yehoshua Gitay (Atlanta: Scholars Press, 1997), 99.

11. I published a sociological interpretation of the Franciscan movement, stressing the insights of Max Weber in Michael Crosby, O.F.M.Cap., *Franciscan Charism* (Pulaski, Wisc.: Franciscan Publishers, 1969). For a more recent application of the "routinization of the charism," see Shanti Abeyashingha, C.Ss.R., "Religious Life and the Max E. Weberian Concept of Bureaucratic Routinization," *Vidyajyoti* 65 (2001): 907–16.

12. Marie Anne Mayeski, " 'Let Women Not Despair': Rabanus Maurus on Women as Prophets," *Theological Studies* 58 (1997): 239.

13. Miriam Therese Winter, "Another Perspective," *The American Catholic*, May 2002, 2. Winter's reference to the "eleven elderly men sequestered together in a room in Rome . . . secretly deciding how the Church will proceed" refers to the April 23–24, 2002, meeting of some leaders of the U.S. hierarchy with Vatican officials (more than eleven total), called by the Vatican to address the pedophilia scandal in the U.S. church.

14. Jerome Murphy-O'Connor, *What Is Religious Life? A Critical Re-Appraisal* (Wilmington, Del.: Michael Glazier, 1977), 13.

15. Pontifical Biblical Commission, "The Interpretation of the Bible in the Church," *Origins* 23 (1994): 510.

16. Murphy-O'Connor, *What Is Religious Life?* 78.

17. Cardinal Walter Kasper, interview with Robert Mickens, "The Whole Truth Is Only Found Together," *The Tablet*, July 6, 2002.

18. I am thankful for being led to this piece of history by Elizabeth A. Dreyer, "Prophetic Voice in Religious Life," *Review for Religious* 62 (2003): 253. Dreyer refers to Mary Catherine Hilkert, O.P., *Speaking with Authority: Catherine of Siena and the Voices of Women Today* (Mahwah, N.J.: Paulist Press, 2001), 43.

19. Karl Rahner, "Do Not Stifle the Spirit," *Theological Investigations* 7 (New York: Herder, 1971), 75–76.

20. Constitutions and Rules of the Congregation of the Missionary Oblates of Mary Immaculate, 9 (Rome: Congregation of the Missionary Oblates of Mary Immaculate, 1982), 21–22.

21. Karl Rahner, "Observations on the Factor of the Charismatic in the Church," *Theological Investigations* 12 (New York: Seabury Press, 1974), 86.

22. Ibid., 94. I am indebted to John Haughey, S.J., for leading me to Rahner in Haughey's "Connecting Vatican II's Call to Holiness with Public Life," *Proceedings of the Fifty-fifth Annual Convention*, Catholic Theological Society of America (CTSA, 2000), 1–19.

23. Haughey, "Connecting Vatican II's Call to Holiness with Public Life," 9.

24. Thomas of Celano, *The Second Life of St. Francis*, 193, in *St. Francis of Assisi: Writings and Early Biographies*, English Omnibus of the Sources for the Life of St. Francis, ed. Marion A. Habig (Chicago: Franciscan Herald Press, 1972), 517.

25. Couturier's findings reinforce the groundbreaking data of David Nygren and Miriam Ukeritis in their study of the attitudes of religious toward the ideal of the poor and the reality of identifying with the poor. See David B. Couturier, O.F.M.Cap., "Minority and Poverty Eradication: The International Dimensions of Christ's Compassion in 21st Century Franciscan Communities," Address to the Provincial Chapter of the Society of St. Francis, May 25, 2003, esp. note 35 detailing sources for his findings.

26. Patricia Wittberg, S.C., and Bryan Froehle, "Generation X and Religious Life: New Findings from CARA Studies," *Horizon: The Journal of the National Religious Vocation Conference*, 23, no. 3 (2000).

27. Joan Chittister, O.S.B., *The Fire in These Ashes: A Spirituality of Contemporary Religious Life* (Kansas City, Mo.: Sheed & Ward, 1995), 14–15.

28. For more on this comparison, see my *Franciscan Charism* (Pulaski, Wisc.: Franciscan Press, 1969), 47–51.

29. Chittister, *The Fire in These Ashes*, 16.

30. At least one bishop, Raymond Burke, then of LaCrosse and now of St. Louis, seemed to support Catholics who disagreed with the pope's stance on the war. See Jessica

Bock, "Bishop: It's OK to Disagree with Pope on War," *Wausau Daily Herald,* March 28, 2003, 1A.

31. Janet Malone, C.N.D., Ed.D., "Prophets in Religious Life," *Human Development* 22 (2001): 38.

32. A study of candidates to the Order of Friars Minor ("Franciscans") confirmed the trend toward social conformism, harm avoidance, and a need to "take the safe course in life." See Richard J. Mucowski, O.F.M., "A Psychological Study of Today's Applicants to Male Religious Communities," *CARA Seminary Forum* 11, no. 4 (Winter 1983), 2, passim. I am thankful to my confrere David Couturier, O.F.M.Cap., for pointing out this study.

33. Dean Hoge, "Recent Research Findings Pertaining to the Formation of Religious Priests," presentation at the CMSM Formation for Celibacy Conference, Jacksonville, Florida, January 2003. Again, I am indebted to David Couturier for leading me to this study.

34. Malone, "Prophets in Religious Life," 36.

35. Ibid., 40.

36. Kurien Kunnumpuram, S.J., "Religious as Prophets of the Lord," *Vidyajyoti* 65 (2001), 837. His conclusion is shared by J. Mannath, "The Cost of Discipleship," in CRI National Association Report 2000, 58–61, and George M. Soares-Prabhu, S.J., "Prophetic Communities *of* and *for* the Kingdom: An Interpretation of Religious Life," *Ignis Studies* 1 (1983). He wrote more than twenty years ago: "Religious in India have, I believe, a long way to go before they can claim to be prophetic communities of and for the Kingdom in this vast and complex land, so rich in its long tradition of a profound and pluriform religiosity, so mired down in poverty and oppression. We are still too bland, too conformist, too comfortably secure in our bourgeois mediocrity" (44).

37. The classic anthropological work on transformation of groups is A. F. C. Wallace, "Revitalization Movements," *American Anthropologist* 58 (1956): 264–81.

38. Gerald A. Arbuckle, S.M., "Understanding Refounding and the Role of Conversion," in *Religious Life: Rebirth through Conversion,* ed. Gerald A. Arbuckle, S.M., and David L. Fleming, S.J. (New York: Alba House, 1990), 52–104.

39. Chittister, *The Fire in These Ashes,* vii.

40. Robert N. Bellah, Richard Madsen, William M. Sullivan, Ann Swidler, and Steven M. Tipton, *Habits of the Heart: Individualism and Commitment in American Life* (Berkeley and Los Angeles: University of California Press, 1985), 50.

41. Barbara Fiand, *Refocusing the Vision: Religious Life into the Future* (New York: Crossroad, 1991), 19.

42. David Nygren and Miriam Ukeritis, "Future of Religious Orders in the United States," Executive Summary, *Origins* 22 (1992): 271.

43. Fifth Plenary Council of the Capuchin Franciscan Order, "Our Prophetic Presence in the World," September 1986, 19, in *The Path of Renewal: The Documents of the Five Plenary Councils and the First Assembly of the Order of Capuchin Friars Minor,* ed. Regis J. Armstrong, O.F.M.Cap. (North American Capuchin Conference, n.d.), 117.

44. Edith Wyschogrod, *Saints and Postmodernism: Revisioning Moral Philosophy* (Chicago: University of Chicago Press, 1990), 3.

Chapter 2 / The Mystical/Prophetic Vocation of Isaiah

1. Dan Schutte, "Here I Am, Lord," 291, in *Gather* (Chicago: GIA Publications, Inc., and Phoenix: North American Liturgy Resources, 1988).

2. Peter F. Ellis, C.Ss.R., *The Men and Message of the Old Testament* (Collegeville, Minn.: Liturgical Press, 1963), 279.

3. Evelyn Underhill, *Mystics in the Church* (New York: Schocken Books, 1971), 32–33.

4. St. Francis of Assisi, quoted in Raphael Brown, trans., *Little Flowers of St. Francis*, in *St. Francis of Assisi: Writings and Early Biographies*, English Omnibus of the Sources for the Life of St. Francis, ed. Marion A. Habig, (Chicago: Franciscan Herald Press, 1972), 1448.

5. Barbara Fiand, *Refocusing the Vision: Religious Life into the Future* (New York: Crossroad, 2001), passim, and Diarmuid O'Murchu, M.S.C., *Religious Life: A Prophetic Vision* (Notre Dame, Ind.: Ave Maria, 1991), 23–24.

6. See St. Thomas Aquinas, *Summa Theologica* I, 45, 7, and Pamela Smith, SS.C.M., "Keystones of Environmental Ethics," The Leadership Conference of Women Religious, *The Occasional Papers* 32 (2003): 17.

7. Alexandra Kovats, C.S.J.P., "Re-Visioning the Vows Holistically," in Leadership Conference of Women Religious, *The Occasional Papers*, 23–30.

8. 1971 Synod of Bishops, introduction to "Justice in the World," in Joseph Gremillion, *The Gospel of Peace and Justice: Catholic Social Teaching since Pope John* (Maryknoll, N.Y.: Orbis Books, 1976), 514.

9. Ibid.

10. Adam Clymer, "World Survey Says Negative Views of U.S. Are Rising," *New York Times*, December 5, 2002. R. C. Longworth, "A Nation Alone: Even Our Friends Don't Share America's Image of Itself," *Chicago Tribune*, Perspective Section, December 30, 2001. Both articles based their insights on results in 2001 and 2002 garnered from data from the Pew Research Center.

11. Norbert Lohfink, S.J., "The Kingdom of God and the Economy in the Bible," *Communio* 13 (1986): 225.

12. Michael H. Crosby, "Leviticus 19: Holiness as Separation vs. Holiness as Mercy," in *The Prayer That Jesus Taught Us* (Maryknoll, N.Y.: Orbis Books, 2002), 64–73. See also Crosby, "Matthew's Gospel: The Disciples' Call to Justice," in *The New Testament: Introducing the Way of Discipleship*, ed. Wes Howard-Brook and Sharon H. Ringe (Maryknoll, N.Y.: Orbis Books, 2002), 25–35.

13. Pope John Paul II, *Vita Consecrata*, Apostolic Exhortation on the Consecrated Life, March 25, 1996, 84 (Boston: Pauline Books & Media, 1996), 138.

14. Sandra Schneiders, I.H.M., *Finding the Treasure: Locating Catholic Religious Life in a New Ecclesial and Cultural Context* (New York and Mahwah, N.J.: Paulist Press, 2000), 139.

15. 1971 Synod of Bishops, II, in Gremillion, *The Gospel of Peace and Justice*,.

16. Ibid., 522.

17. Schneiders, *Finding the Treasure*, 333.

18. Joan Chittister, O.S.B., *The Fire in These Ashes: A Spirituality of Contemporary Religious Life* (Kansas City, Mo.: Sheed & Ward, 1995), 10–11.

19. Pope John Paul II, *Vita Consecrata*, 85, 138.

20. For more on this see John W. Miller: *Meet the Prophets: A Beginner's Guide to the Books of the Biblical Prophets* (New York and Mahwah, N.J.: Paulist Press, 1987), 20–25.

21. Abraham J. Heschel, *The Prophets: An Introduction* (New York: Harper & Row Torchbooks, 1969), 202.

22. St. Francis of Assisi, "Testament," in *St. Francis of Assisi: Writings and Early Biographies*, 67.

23. St. Clare of Assisi, "The Testament of Saint Clare," 7, in *Francis and Clare: The Complete Works*, Classics of Western Spirituality, trans. and ed. Regis J. Armstrong, O.F.M.Cap., and Ignatius C. Brady, O.F.M. (New York: Paulist Press, 1982), 228.

24. Abraham J. Heschel, *The Prophets: An Introduction* (New York: Harper & Row Torchbooks, 1969), 90.

25. 1971 Synod of Bishops, "Justice in the World," III, in Joseph Gremillion, *The Gospel of Peace and Justice: Catholic Social Teaching since Pope John* (Maryknoll, N.Y.: Orbis Books, 1976), 523–4.

26. Ibid.

27. Pope John Paul II, *Vita Consecrata*, Apostolic Exhortation on the Consecrated Life, 86, 140, 139.

28. Sandra M. Schneiders, I.H.M., *Selling All: Commitment, Consecrated Celibacy, and Community in Catholic Religious Life* (New York: Paulist Press, 2001), 221.

29. Pope Paul VI, *Evangelica Testificatio*, Apostolic Exhortation on the Renewal of the Religious Life according to the Teachings of the Second Vatican Council, June 29, 1971, 18 (Washington, D.C.: United States Catholic Conference, 1971), 7.

30. Ibid.

31. Patricia Wittberg, S.C., "The Problem of Generations in Religious Life," *Review for Religious* (1988): 905–11.

32. Walter Brueggemann, *The Prophetic Imagination*, 2nd ed. (Minneapolis: Fortress, 2001), xvi.

Chapter 3 / Jeremiah and the Scroll: The Need to Be Formed in the Word

1. Abraham J. Heschel, *The Prophets: An Introduction* (New York: Harper Torchbooks, 1962), 12.

2. Mary C. Carroll, S.S.S.F., "Jeremiah Speaking Today," *Human Development* 23 (Winter 2002): 9.

3. Meister Eckhart in Matthew Fox, *Breakthrough* (Garden City, N.Y.: Image, 1980), 59.

4. Heschel, *The Prophets: An Introduction*, 25–26.

5. Walter Brueggemann, *The Prophetic Imagination*, 2nd ed. (Minneapolis: Fortress, 2001), 46.

6. For more on these notions, see my *Rethinking Celibacy, Reclaiming the Church* (Eugene, Ore.: Wipf and Stock, 2003).

7. Heschel, *The Prophets: An Introduction*, 121.

8. This is how I interpret the statement of Bishop Wilton Gregory, the past president of the United States Conference of Catholic Bishops. Upon release of two studies on the sexual abuse of children by more than four thousand priests, he said: "The terrible history recorded here today is history." Bishop Gregory was quoted in Laurie Goodstein, "Abuse Scandal Is Now 'History,' Top Bishop Says," *New York Times*, February 28, 2004.

9. Walter Brueggemann, *Texts That Linger: Words That Explode: Listening to Prophetic Voices*, ed. Patrick D. Miller (Minneapolis: Fortress, 2000), 8.

10. Ibid.

11. Walter Brueggemann, *Deep Memory, Exuberant Hope: Contested Truth in a Post-Christian World* (Minneapolis: Fortress, 2000), 15.

12. Edward W. Said, "Intellectual Exile: Expatriates and Marginals," in Said, *Representations of the Intellectual*, 1993 Reith Lectures (New York: Pantheon Books, 1994), 52–53.

13. Brueggemann, *Texts that Linger*, 9.

14. Thomas of Celano, *The First Life of St. Francis of Assisi*, 8, in *St. Francis of Assisi: Writings and Early Biographies*, English Omnibus of the Sources for the Life of St. Francis, ed. Marion A. Habig (Chicago: Franciscan Herald Press, 1972), 236.

15. Ibid., 7, 235.

16. Thomas of Celano, *The Second Life of St. Francis of Assisi*, 105, in *St. Francis of Assisi: Writings and Early Biographies*, 448.

17. The Rule, 1, in *The Rule and Life of the Brothers and Sisters of the Third Order Regular of St. Francis and Commentary* (Washington, D.C.: Franciscan Federation Third Order Regular of the Sisters and Brothers of the United States, 1982/1997), 19.

18. An example of this can be found in the way church governance has come to be dominated by the male, celibate, clerical caste by an appeal to Matthew 16:17–19.

19. Pope John Paul II, *Vita Consecrata*, 94 (Boston: Pauline Books & Media, 1996), 150–51.

20. Heschel, *The Prophets II* (New York: Harper Torchbooks, 1962), 5.

21. Ibid., 11.

22. John Bright, *The Kingdom of God* (New York and Nashville: Abingdon Press Paperback, 1953), 119–20.

23. Heschel, *The Prophets: An Introduction*, 3–4.

24. Ibid., 4–5.

25. Brueggemann, *The Prophetic Imagination*, 47.

26. Carroll, "Jeremiah Speaking Today," 12.

Chapter 4 / Ezekiel as Exile

1. In my reflections I have been helped much by Daniel L. Smith, *The Religion of the Landless: The Social Context of the Babylonian Exile* (Bloomington, Ind.: Meyer-Stone, 1989).

2. According to the Jewish historian Jacob Neusner, the Exile itself was the seminal experience that sculpted other key parts of the Old Testament, including the Pentateuch itself, especially in its Priestly version: "The Pentateuch in these ways laid emphasis upon serving God through sacrifice in the Temple, conducted by the priests, and upon Israel's living a holy way of life as a 'kingdom of priests and a holy people' — all in accord with God's message to Moses at Sinai. But of course 'Sinai' stood for Babylonia. In Babylonia the priests drew together the elements of the received picture and reshaped them into the fairly coherent set of rules and narratives we now know as the Pentateuch" (*Self-Fulfilling Prophecies: Exile and Return in the History of Judaism* [Boston: Beacon, 1988], 33).

3. Walter Brueggemann, "A Shattered Transcendence? Exile and Restoration," in *Biblical Theology: Problems and Perspectives*, ed. Steven J. Kraftchick, Charles D. Myers, and Ben C. Ollenburger (Nashville: Abingdon, 1995), 169.

4. Smith, *The Religion of the Landless*, 214.

5. Edward W. Said, "Reflections on Exile," in *Reflections on Exile and Other Essays* (Cambridge, Mass.: Harvard University Press 2001), 184.

6. In its broadest definition "spirituality" involves "the experience of the transcendent that is expressed in one's life in the context of community." For Christians this is further

specified as "the experience of the trinitarian God revealed in Jesus Christ that is expressed in worship and works in the context of a community of disciples." For some it might be translated as "the communal celebration of the faith that does justice."

7. Paul Joyce, *Divine Initiative and Human Response in Ezekiel,* Journal for the Study of the Old Testament, Supplement 51 (Sheffield: Billings and Sons, 1989), 16.

8. Richard P. McBrien, "Rumblings on the Right," *Milwaukee Catholic Herald,* April 8, 2002.

9. Richard John Neuhaus, "Scandal Time," Public Square, *First Things* 122 (April 2002): 63.

10. Eugene Cullen Kennedy, "Fall From Grace: Abuse Scandals Strain an Already Crumbling Institution," *National Catholic Reporter,* March 8, 2002.

11. Bruce Vawter and Leslie J. Hoppe, *Ezekiel: A New Heart,* International Theological Commentary (Grand Rapids: Wm. B. Eerdmans and Edinburgh: Handsel Press, 1991), 17.

12. Mary Douglas, quoted in Smith, *The Religion of the Landless,* 82.

13. David R. Carlin Jr., "Don't Tear Down Fences: First Ask Why They Are There," *Commonweal* 74 (July 18, 1997): 10.

14. Walter J. Brueggemann, *Hopeful Imagination* (Philadelphia: Fortress, 1988), 57.

15. Ezekiel 22:26 declares: "Its priests have done violence to my teaching and have profaned my holy things; they have made no distinction between the holy and the common, neither have they taught the difference between the unclean and the clean, and they have disregarded my sabbaths, so that I am profaned among them."

16. Vawter and Hoppe, *Ezekiel: A New Heart,* 55.

17. Brueggemann, *Hopeful Imagination,* 86.

18. Ibid., 82.

19. Vawter and Hoppe, *Ezekiel: A New Heart,* 83.

20. Brueggemann, *Hopeful Imagination,* 72–73.

21. Tamara C. Eskenazi, "Exile and the Dreams of Return," *Currents in Theology and Mission* 17 (1990): 194.

22. Said, *Reflections on Exile,* 173.

23. Thomas of Celano, "The Second Life of St. Francis," 125, in *St. Francis of Assisi: Writings and Early Biographies,* 466. For an elaboration on the connection between Francis and Ezekiel 24, see Auspicius van Corstanje, O.F.M., *The Third Order for Our Times* (Chicago: Franciscan Herald Press, 1974), 113–17.

24. Vawter and Hoppe, *Ezekiel: A New Heart,* 14.

25. Reed Abelson, "Study Finds Bias on the Job Is Still Common," *New York Times,* July 24, 2002.

26. Said, *Reflections on Exile,* 180.

27. According to the Old Testament scholar Dianne Bergant, C.S.A., what probably occurred was that the once-dominant goddess images of the Canaanites, from which Israel had never been purified, came to greater expression. Private conversation with the author, November 14, 1997.

28. Dianne Bergant, C.S.A., "Compassion in the Bible," in *Compassionate Ministry,* ed. Gary L. Sapp (Birmingham: Religious Education Press, 1993), 12.

29. Ibid., 10.

30. Alice Walker, *The Color Purple* (New York: Washington Square Press, 1982), 177, 178.

31. For a good summary of papal statements on political economy see John T. Pawlikowski, O.S.M., "Papal Teaching on Economic Justice: Change and Continuity," *New Theology Review* 10 (1997): 60–77.

32. For more on this see James Twitchell, *Lead Us into Temptation: The Triumph of American Materialism* (New York: Columbia University Press, 1999).

33. Said, *Reflections on Exile*, 179.

34. Brueggemann, *The Prophetic Imagination*, 76.

35. Brueggemann, *Hopeful Imagination*, 66.

36. Charles Péguy, "Hope," in *God Speaks*, trans. Julian Green (New York: Pantheon, 1965), 93.

Chapter 5 / The Prophetic Witness of Non-Assent and Non-Submission

1. Synod of Bishops, Second General Assembly, "Justice in the World," introduction, in Joseph Gremillion, *The Gospel of Peace and Justice: Catholic Social Teaching since Pope John* (Maryknoll, N.Y.: Orbis Books, 1976), 514.

2. H. D. Thoreau, "Civil Disobedience," in *The Selected Works of Thoreau*, ed. Walter Harding (Boston: Houghton Mifflin, 1975).

3. John Rawls, *A Theory of Justice* (Cambridge, Mass.: The Belknap Press of Harvard University, 1971), 364.

4. Kathy Kiely, "Abortion Battle Hits Pivotal Point," *USA Today*, January 16, 2003.

5. Administrative Committee, National Conference of Catholic Bishops, "Pastoral Message [on Abortion]," February 13, 1973.

6. Sacred Congregation for the Doctrine of Faith, "Declaration on Procured Abortion" (St. Paul: Wanderer Press, 1974), 22.

7. Michael H. Crosby, O.F.M.Cap., "Religious Life: A Prophetic Voice in the Midst of Violence," Workshop at Joint Assembly, LCWR and CMSM, August 21, 2004.

8. The Sacred Congregation for the Doctrine of the Faith, "Declaration on Procured Abortion," 18.

9. "Vatican Rejects Capuchin Election," Briefs, *National Catholic Reporter*, August 2, 2002, 10.

10. Lawrence S. Cunningham, "Conscience and Dissent: What is the Place of Dissent in the Church?" *U.S. Catholic* (July 2003), 29.

11. Sr. Christine Vladimiroff, O.S.B., "Response" to Reception of Call to Action's Leadership Award, November 3, 2002, in Terry Dosh, *Bread Rising* 13, no. 1 (2003), 1.

12. Second Vatican Council, *Lumen Gentium*, 12, in Walter M. Abbott, S.J., general editor, *The Documents of Vatican II* (New York: Guild Press, 1966), 29.

13. John E. Thiel, "Tradition and Authoritative Reasoning: A Nonfoundationalist Perspective," *Theological Studies* 56 (1995): 630.

14. Ibid., 631.

15. Ibid., 650–51.

16. Barbara Fiand, *Refocusing the Vision: Religious Life into the Future* (New York: Crossroad, 2001), 164.

17. *Lumen Gentium*, 34; *Gaudium et Spes*, 16.

18. James P. Hanigan, "Conscience and the Holy Spirit," in *Proceedings,* 51st Annual Convention, Catholic Theological Society of America, 1996 (New York: St. John's University, 1996), 236.

19. Ibid., 237.

20. Ibid., 238–39.

21. Pontifical Biblical Commission, "The Interpretation of the Bible in the Church," III, *Origins* 23 (1993): 513.

22. Hanigan, "Conscience and the Holy Spirit," 242.

23. Ibid., 243. Here Hanigan refers to the teaching of Pope John Paul II in *Dominum et Vivificantem,* 46. I do not think the pope is making the same conclusions in his encyclical about the Spirit at work in the faithful as Hanigan is!

24. Pope Paul VI, Apostolic Exhortation *Evangelica Testificatio,* 18 (Washington, D.C.: USCC Publications Office, 1971), 7.

25. Karl Rahner, "Do Not Stifle the Spirit," in *Theological Investigations* 7 (New York: Herder, 1971), 82.

26. Ibid., 83.

27. Ibid., 85.

28. Ibid., 84.

29. Joan Chittister, O.S.B., *The Fire in These Ashes: A Spirituality of Contemporary Religious Life* (Kansas City, Mo.: Sheed & Ward, 1995), 3.

30. Sister Christine Vladimiroff, O.S.B., "Regarding Deliberations with the Vatican," in *The American Catholic* (June–July 2001): 5.

31. As an example see Kathleen Long, O.P., *Proclaiming Truth through Non-Violent Dissent: Working to Close the U.S. Army School of the Americas* (Chicago: Catholic Theological Union, 2002).

32. "Bd. Mary McKillop," in Robert Ellsberg, *All Saints: Daily Reflections on Saints, Prophets, and Witnesses for Our Time* (New York: Crossroad, 1997), 335.

33. Francis of Assisi, "Testament," in *Francis and Clare: The Complete Works.* Classics of Western Spirituality, trans. and ed. Regis J. Armstrong, O.F.M.Cap. and Ignatius Brady, O.F.M. (New York: Paulist Press, 1982), 154.

34. Thomas of Celano, *The Second Life of St. Francis* 10, *St. Francis of Assisi: Writings and Early Biographies,* ed. Marion A. Habig (Chicago: Franciscan Herald Press, 1972), 370.

35. Thadée Matura, O.F.M., "The Church in the Writings of St. Francis of Assisi," trans. Helen Eckrich, O.S.F., *Greyfriars Review* 12 (1998), 31.

36. A good amount of the material that follows can be found in Michael H. Crosby, O.F.M.Cap., "'Francis, Repair My House,'" *The Cord* 47 (1997): 102–19.

37. Arnaldo Fortini, *Francis of Assisi,* trans. Helen Moak (New York: Crossroad, 1981), 295.

38. Francis of Assisi, quoted in Celano, *Second Life,* 148, in *St. Francis of Assisi: Writings and Early Biographies,* 481–82. The bishop became Pope Gregory IX.

39. Francis of Assisi, "The First Version of the Letter to the Faithful," 48–53, in Armstrong and Brady, *Francis and Clare,* 70. Essential elements of this are repeated in his "First Version" as well (5–7, 63). The notions also are found in the "Earlier Rule," 22, 27–31.

40. Francis of Assisi, quoted in *The Legend of Perugia,* 114, in *St. Francis of Assisi: Writings and Early Biographies,* 1088–89.

41. Francis of Assisi, "The Later Rule," 1, in Armstrong and Brady, *Francis and Clare,* 137.

42. Ibid., X, 142.

43. Some say the "privilege of poverty" was not the only conflict experienced by Clare with the Benedictine Rule. Some say she had difficulties with a form of authority that stressed the superior to the detriment of the Spirit working among the members and from an overly restrictive approach to the enclosure. See Sr. Madge Karecki, S.S.J-T.O.S.F., "Clare and Conflict," *The Cord* 33 (1993): 51–55.

44. Ingrid J. Petersen, O.S.F., *Clare of Assisi: A Biographical Study* (Quincy, Ill.: Franciscan Press, 1993), 168.

45. Aidan McGraith, O.F.M., "Between Charism and Institution: The Approval of the Rule of Saint Clare in 1253," *Greyfriars Review* 13 (1999): 199–200.

46. Clare of Assisi, "The Rule of St. Clare," 3, in Armstrong and Brady, *Francis and Clare*, 211.

47. Ibid., 1–2.

48. I find it interesting that these same sentiments seemed to undergird the famous intervention of Cardinal Lecaro during the Second Vatican Council. In his mind, only when the Church would become poor and in solidarity with the poor would it be transformed. His words, we know, fell on deaf ears.

49. For more background on this notion, see Caroline Walker Bynum, *Holy Feast and Holy Fast: The Religious Significance of Food to Medieval Women* (Berkeley: University of California Press, 1987).

50. For a good elaboration on the dynamics of Clare's resistance, see Gigismund Verhij, "Personal Awareness of Vocation and Ecclesiastical Authority as Exemplified in St. Clare of Assisi," trans. Ignatius McCormick, O.F.M.Cap., *Greyfriars Review* 3 (1989): 35–42.

51. Francis of Assisi, quoted in "The Rule of St. Clare," VI, in Armstrong and Brady, *Francis and Clare*, 218.

52. Francis of Assisi, "Last Will" for Clare, in *St. Francis of Assisi: Writings and Early Biographies*, 76. Emphasis added.

53. Thomas of Celano, *First Life*, 8, in *St. Francis of Assisi: Writings and Early Biographies*, 236.

54. Francis of Assisi, in Armstrong and Brady, *Francis and Clare*, 154–55.

55. Clare of Assisi, "The Second Letter to Blessed Agnes of Prague," 15, in Armstrong and Brady, *Francis and Clare*, 197. This letter is placed in 1235–36.

56. Francis of Assisi, "Final Rule," X, in Armstrong and Brady, *Francis and Clare*, 144. This notion is used various times in Francis's writings. See Admonition I, no. 1; "The First Version of the Letter to the Faithful," n. 3.

57. Hanigan, "Conscience and the Holy Spirit," 246.

58. Francis of Assisi, "Final Rule," X, in Armstrong and Brady, *Francis and Clare*, 143.

59. Hanigan, "Conscience and the Holy Spirit," 244–45.

60. McGraith, "Between Charism and Institution," 200.

61. Francis of Assisi, "Testament," 6–10, in Armstrong and Brady, *Francis and Clare*, 154.

62. Hanigan, "Conscience and the Holy Spirit," 245.

63. 1971 Synod of Bishops, III, "Justice in the World," 41, in Gremillion, *The Gospel of Peace and Justice*, 522.

64. Sacred Congregation for the Doctrine of Faith, "Declaration on Procured Abortion," 18.

65. Jeremiah Crosby, O.F.M.Cap., *Bearing Witness: The Place of the Franciscan Family in the Church* (Chicago: Franciscan Herald Press, 1965), 12.

Guide for Reflection

Many small groups and communities are using the material in this book for private and communal reflection. Here are some questions that might enliven conversation and help readers apply the ideas to their own lives personally, communally, and institutionally.

1. Review Michael Crosby's explanation of the Church of Matthew 16 and the Church of Matthew 18 (p. 37). Name the qualities that are associated with each type. What tensions might exist between the two ways of seeing the church? What qualities are most characteristic of your own community and the communities around you? Of the church as a whole?

2. "Once we experience the reign, the realm, the reality, and indeed the rush of God's presence and power breaking into our lives, all else becomes relativized, an illusion" (p. 63).

   Has there been a time when you or someone in your community experienced this "rush" of God's presence? What were the circumstances? How did the experience influence your lives? Did this experience help you see the levels of "the world" in another way?

3. "Jeremiah was called to celibacy, and his specific witness was meant to serve as a symbolic protest against the infidelity of his people. In this light, therefore, I hold that unless our call to celibacy is manifested as part of the deeper dimension of prophetic protest, our celibacy will not likely be either healthy or countercultural" (p. 89).

   Like many other heated issues, celibacy is much debated in our world today. (If you have taken a vow of celibacy:) Reflect on your own life of celibacy. Do you find that it is rooted in the "deeper dimension" Crosby identifies here? If so, how? (If you are not celibate:) Reflect on celibacy among religious. How do you experience that part of their Christian witness? Does it challenge and enrich your life? Discuss how, if so.

4. "Despite significant statements from the pope on the 'savagery' of our capitalist brand of political economy, too often we, the church, represent the managerial and business class and subscribe uncritically to its interests" (p. 132).

   Reflect on the economic aspect of prophetic life. Can you think of examples from your church and community of ways that people successfully challenge the excesses of capitalism? How might you apply some of these practices in your own life personally, communally, and congregationally?

5. "The appeal to the Spirit, invoked by the brothers in their previous election, cannot be taken lightly nor can it be reduced to a simple 'our' Spirit vs. 'their' Spirit difference. The fact that both a group like ours and the decision-makers in the Vatican claim the Spirit's guidance must not be taken lightly, especially when conflicts arise in a noninfallible teaching or discipline" (p. 155 153)

   Reflect on the issue of conflicts in religious orders and in the institutional church. Think about experiences of conflict you have witnessed or participated in. What do conflicting views of guidance from the Spirit suggest about the nature of the Spirit? What ways can you identify for communities to reflect on spiritual inspiration when disagreements arise?

6. Reflect and comment on Crosby's thoughts about Isaiah, the priest assumed to be holy, who had the mystical experience showing him how sinful he and his society were vis-à-vis God's holiness. How does the "Holy Trinity" invite us to a new way of seeing sin?

Other ideas for reflection

"Authentic prophecy flows from the mystical experience; the mystical experience is empty without its proclamation in prophecy" (p. 14).

"Why might some religious act very prophetically but in ways often isolated from and even rejected by the wider membership?" (p. 17).

"If our members have never sufficiently embraced the notion of being 'prophetic,' it is little wonder that efforts to promote the prophetic dimension of religious life face resistance or defiance " (p. 48).

"Too often conversion has been thought of as a 'turning away.' Isaiah's conversion was different, a resounding 'yes' rather than a simple 'no'" (p. 69)

Of Related Interest

Barbara Fiand
REFOCUSING THE VISION
Religious Life into the Future

"My last ten years' encounter with religious life, especially through my retreat and workshop ministry, has deeply enriched me, but has also increased my sense of urgency to bring things out into the open, to identify disagreements and encourage discussion, to invite us to come together in order to face the struggle that all of us are experiencing." — *From the Preface*

0-8245-1890-X, $18.95 paperback

Diarmuid O'Murchu
POVERY, CELIBACY, AND OBEDIENCE
A Radical Option for Life

"A strong book, a daring call to relevance, a deep ground of religious life in humankind's holiest tradition." — *Barbara Fiand*

0-8245-1473-4, $14.95 paperback

Dean Brackley, S.J.
THE CALL TO DISCERNMENT IN TROUBLED TIMES
New Perspectives on the Transformative Wisdom of Ignatius of Loyola

As the centerpiece of Crossroad's expanding offerings in Jesuit spirituality and thought, we offer this remarkable book from Dean Brackley, a leader in social justice movements and professor in El Salvador. Brackley takes us through the famous Ignatian exercises, showing that they involve not only private religious experience but also a social, moral dimension, including the care for others.

0-8245-2268-0, $24.95 paperback

crossroad

Of Related Interest

Michael Crosby
SOLANUS CASEY
The Official Account of a Virtuous American Life

"This volume makes public the simple yet awesome facts of a man whose relationship with God was so profound that his prayers could help heal people."
— *New York Times*

In 1995, Pope John Paul II bestowed on Bernard (Solanus) Casey the title of
Venerable, making him the first male born in the U.S. to be elevated to this
position. This true story of an American saint, excerpted from the official
1300-page canonization document, is both a moving spiritual biography and
an inside look at the canonization process.

0-8245-1835-7, $19.95 paperback

Please support your local bookstore,
or call 1-800-707-0670 for Customer Service.

For a free catalog, write us at

THE CROSSROAD PUBLISHING COMPANY
16 Penn Plaza, 481 Eighth Avenue
New York, NY 10001

Visit our website at
www.crossroadpublishing.com
All prices subject to change.

crossroad